Marriage Uncounseling

A Counterintuitive Approach
to Healing Relationships and
Bringing Back Love

Liam Naden

Growing in Love for Life Publishing

ISBN: 978-1-9911909-5-6 Paperback
ISBN: 978-1-9911909-3-2 Hardcover
ISBN: 978-1-9911909-8-7 eBook
ISBN: 978-1-9911909-0-1 Audio

Author's Note

Some of the material for this book was originally contained in the podcast 'Growing in Love for Life: Save and Heal Your Marriage' which can be listened to online at https://growinginloveforlife.com/podcasts/

Subsequently this content was also used in the Growing in Love for Life e-book series which can be found here: https://www.amazon.com/dp/B074CBBQQ1

*One of life's greatest gifts is a
truly loving marriage.*

*But you cannot buy it or
bargain for it. You can only be
worthy of receiving it.*

Contents

Special Free Bonuses

As a thank-you for purchasing this book I have included some very special bonuses. These will help you to heal your marriage even faster.

Bonuses include:

The Ultimate Love Letter Collection

A letter to your spouse – using the right words – can be one of the most powerful and effective ways to achieve a breakthrough in your marriage.
Each of these letters contains specific phrases and ideas designed to give you those breakthroughs.

- Love Letter #1: To re-activate the attraction between you

- Love Letter #2: To heal the hurt and create true forgiveness

- Love Letter #3: To open up honest communication

- Love Letter #4: To show true love and appreciation

- Love Letter #5: To get them to commit to your marriage (even if they are leaving or have left)

These - and other - bonuses are exclusive to this book (you won't find them anywhere else).

You will find all the details for accessing all of them at the end of the book.

Introduction

If you are struggling with problems in your marriage, you will know that nothing has the power to make you more miserable.

After all, the state of your marriage has more of an impact on the quality of your life than virtually anything else.

You can have it all: health, wealth and fame. But if your marriage isn't happy then you won't be happy either.

Conversely, everything can be going wrong in your life, but even if you're sick and penniless, having a loving partner to support you and share your journey will make everything seem bearable and even worthwhile.

But how do you create that wonderful marriage - the one you signed up for when you exchanged your wedding vows? And what do you do to get over the problems that show up which block you from achieving it?

Usually the first reaction, when a problem appears, is to work on the problem to try to fix it.

But even if you solve the problem (which often doesn't happen, despite a large amount of effort and struggle), more problems keep showing up.

And no matter how hard you try, your marriage situation just doesn't improve. In fact, it may feel like things are only getting worse.

Counseling, reading books, trying new ideas, long conversations with your spouse, asking friends, trying to 'think positive' and even showering your spouse with love.....

No matter what you do, you can't achieve that significant breakthrough to heal your marriage and create the deep and lasting intimacy and connection that you crave.

So you begin to believe that the answer lies in trying even harder.

But trying harder to solve your problems is not the answer to achieving a happy marriage.

This may seem like a very controversial statement. But, in this book, you will discover that it is absolutely true. You will realize that the secret to building a truly loving marriage is to do something else entirely.

You will learn here an approach to healing your marriage that you probably haven't heard of before. I have used it to help thousands of people improve their marriages, and even stop divorce.

Many of these people had 'tried' for decades to solve their marital problems.

But it was only when they realized that 'trying' and focusing on their problems was actually at the root of their marriage issues that they finally started to experience breakthroughs.

In this book you'll learn the real reasons why trying to solve the problems in your marriage won't heal your marriage and what to do instead.

You'll understand why counseling may not have been helpful for you and may even have been counterproductive.

I believe that it is possible to heal and transform virtually any marriage, no matter what state it is in.

But only - and this is a big but - **only** if at least **one** of the individuals in the marriage does the **right** things.

In the **right** way, and in the **right** order.

This book will show you the right things - how to do them, and in the right way and in the right order.

So, if you've tried counseling, talking to your spouse and other ways to try to fix the problems and you are still not where you want to be in your marriage - it's time for a new approach: ***Un*counseling**.

With Uncounseling, some of the ideas and concepts may, on the surface, seem counterintuitive. But once you dig a little deeper, you'll realize that this new approach to healing your marriage is not only logical, but obvious.

You'll wonder why you'd never thought of it before.

My sincerest wish for you is the gift of a loving marriage. It's one of the keys to true happiness in your life, and it's what you deserve to have.

How to Use This Book

I should alert you now:

This book is going to require you to **think**.

To think about your marriage. To think about your spouse.

But, above all, to think about **yourself**.

Because **you** are the key to your marriage success.

In each chapter you will find new ideas, questions and exercises that will get you thinking. They will help you understand and apply what you really need to heal and build a wonderful marriage.

I encourage you to answer the questions and engage fully with the exercises. They are not difficult. But it is essential for you to complete them in order to get the best results.

You will also notice a certain degree of repetition of ideas, albeit within different contexts. This is intentional.

Strengthening your marriage, and overcoming problems, only requires you do a few things - but you must do them well.

By learning and applying the concepts of Uncounseling in different ways (as explained in the different chapters) they are much more likely to become a part of your life - and therefore give you the results you want.

I have also deliberately not filled this book out with success stories of others who have used the ideas presented here.

Other than making the book longer, that would only serve to take the focus away from you and your own marriage situation.

Finally, this is a book to nibble on rather than devour in one go.

You may be facing a crisis in your marriage and wanting a solution as quickly as possible.

However, you will receive the best results by taking the process of Uncounseling one step at a time.

Consider the information presented here and complete the exercises. You also might find it useful to have something handy to make notes with, to record the ideas and thoughts that come to you as you are reading.

Take small actions and keep going....

By doing so you will get results that will surprise and delight you.

Chapter 1: Where to Start to Finally Heal Your Marriage

In our modern society it seems that most people have problems in their marriage or relationship.

Many have big issues and are facing traumas and the real possibility of their marriage ending. The high divorce rate is one of the tragedies of life today.

However, with the right tools and strategies it doesn't need to be this way.

There are two things I have come to realize that are highly significant about marriages and relationships:

1. Your marriage will have a greater influence on your happiness and the quality of your life than anything else.

The results may be negative or positive, but what you experience in your life is going to be determined to a very large degree by the quality of your relationship.

No matter how independent you think you are, there is no escaping this. And it's actually a very good thing, as marriage gives you a unique opportunity to discover some of the most meaningful aspects of being a human being.

2. No matter how 'successful' you may be in any other area of your life - be it financial, business, health, career or anything else - you will never be *truly* successful until you master the ability to create a satisfying intimate relationship with another person.

This means you need to master the skills of relationships. That is what this book is designed to help you to do.

* * *

My approach to helping people to create successful marriages has essentially come from three sources.

Firstly, over the years I have done a lot of work in the areas of personal development, self-help, peak performance and human motivation. I have taken some of the most effective ideas from these fields and applied them to the area of marriage and intimate relationships.

Secondly, I have learned through trial and error what works and what doesn't. This has come through my own personal experience, and through helping other couples and individuals with their own marriages.

Thirdly - and in some ways this is the most interesting and important - I have made a study of other marriages. I've seen that there are essentially two types of marriage:

Firstly, there are what I call **Low-Intensity Marriages**. These may have been exciting once, but over time the intensity has diminished.

The couple are still together, but their marriage is not passionate. They no longer experience the joy and intimacy that they did early on in their marriage.

These marriages usually have problems, stress and dissatisfaction. And if and when the couple try to solve their problems, their efforts generally create more of the same.

The couple stumbles along, in the belief that problems are 'a natural part of married life.'

If these marriages don't dissolve into divorce (which statistics show the majority do) then they certainly aren't fulfilling and wonderfully happy for the two people involved.

Unfortunately, this is the majority of marriages today.

However, there is another group of people who have a very different type of marriage - what I call **High-Intensity Marriages**. This is a much smaller group than the first, but it is extremely interesting.

In this category are couples who might have been together for quite some time, yet no matter how long they've been married, the intensity of their love has remained.

Theirs is a rich and fulfilling marriage. They adore and worship each other. They hang out together. They are best friends. They laugh together. They have a lot of fun.

It seems that none of the passion and joy has gone from their marriage at all. In fact, it only seems to have gotten better with time.

These couples don't have a relationship dominated by problems or stress.

And they're not struggling to keep their marriage alive, let alone flourishing.

Although this is a much smaller group, it does prove that it *is* possible to create a marriage that keeps getting better with time.

However, for that to happen, the people in this group obviously must be doing something quite different to the majority. As it turns out, they are.

By studying and comparing these two types of marriage (and applying some of my own knowledge of human behavior and my experience), I began to observe patterns. And I discovered that there are clear patterns of success and failure when it comes to marriage.

One thing I realized early on was that what actually 'works' in creating a great marriage (and keeping it that way) is rather different to what most people think.

Most people think that a marriage is something you have to 'work at'. And they think that problems need to be 'worked on'.

They think that by 'working on their problems', they will be able to 'solve' those problems, and that their marriage will be better as a result.

But the problems in your marriage are not the problem! Problems are merely the manifestation of something deeper. **Problems are not the *cause* of an unhappy or unfulfilling marriage, they are the *result* of one.**

The only way to truly heal a marriage is to uncover - and remove - the underlying **causes** of **why** the marriage isn't functioning well. Once that happens, the problems will be resolved by themselves.

To illustrate what I mean by this, think about a pain you might experience in your body. If you were to seek the help of someone skilled in understanding how the human body works, you would find that their approach would not be to try to get rid of your symptom directly; they wouldn't just give you some pain killers and send you home!

Instead, they would try to find the **cause** of the pain. This would involve looking at what is going on inside your body. It may be that one of your organs is not functioning correctly. It may be that your body is out of alignment, which is why you have that pain in your hip or your knee.

But whatever it is, once they identified and rectified the cause of your pain, that pain would disappear.

The same is true of relationships. Once you identify and rectify the cause of a problem, the pain itself (the problem) disappears.

This approach is very effective. Ultimately, it is the only way you can achieve a pain-free marriage.

It does not involve sitting down and talking about individual problems and trying to find a solution for them.

It's not about applying a 'problem solving' method or technique.

Instead, it's about dealing with the 'internal functioning' of your relationship and letting the problems solve themselves.

This approach is what Uncounseling - and this book - is all about.

* * *

We live in a very different world to that of our grandparents. Life and relationships today are far too complex to use such a simplistic approach as 'working on the problems.'

In the 21st century we need a different approach. We need a new way of dealing with the expectations and pressures that modern society now places upon us.

The old approach of simply working on the problems doesn't work anymore, if indeed it ever did.

The Shattered Dreams of Marriage

What happened when you and your spouse first met?

Obvious as it sounds, everything started with attraction. You both found each other interesting - even fascinating - on all sorts of levels.

You fell in love. And all the fun and pleasure that you experienced as a result led you to the desire to form a deep and lasting relationship.

In the beginning, everything was new and exciting. You were both putting a lot of effort into your relationship because it felt so good being around each other.

As things developed further you came to a point where you decided:

"This is the person I want to spend the rest of my life with."

And your decision turned into a commitment we call 'marriage'.

Along with that commitment came an expectation that all the wonderful feelings that you were experiencing were going to continue and get even better.

It was a time of anticipation, optimism and joy.

But, looking at things objectively, isn't it rather odd that you should have been so full of hope and optimism - and even got married at all - when the statistics show that your marriage was unlikely to succeed in the long term?

The divorce rate is around 50% for first marriages and it's even higher for second and third marriages. But of course, when you decided to marry, the prospect of failure probably didn't occur to you.

You were determined that your marriage would succeed - you were committed to 'making it work'.

Unfortunately, if you are like most couples, the great start didn't continue. Other things came into your life: children, a home, career or a business.

All of these probably came or developed after your marriage did and they all needed time and attention - time and attention that was inevitably diverted away from your relationship.

So your marriage got pushed down the list of your priorities. Even if you didn't intend or want this to happen, in most cases, it's just what happened.

Other things in your life became more pressing and urgent to deal with than your marriage relationship.

And it's at about this time that problems started to appear in your marriage.

They may have begun as small things, things that you accepted as natural - and which didn't seem that important.

But over time the small issues gradually turned into big problems. You may also have faced major challenges along the way - the deaths of loved ones, or adverse changes in your finances, career or living situation.

There may have even been direct challenges to your marriage such as an affair.

All of these 'life events' had a detrimental effect on your marriage - to the point where you eventually came to realize that your marriage was simply not providing you with the love, intimacy and sheer pleasure that it once did.

Today, far from being loving and exciting, your marriage may seem uninteresting, irritating or even painful.

All of this may leave you feeling sad, distressed, fearful - and above all powerless to know what to do to bring all those good feelings back.

One of the main purposes of this book is to help you understand what causes a marriage to get to this point.

Because once you do, you can begin to steer your own marriage back in the right direction - to fulfil all the hopes and dreams you had for your marriage when you started on the journey.

A First Step for Healing Your Marriage

Here's something to try with your spouse right away that will make a big difference. It's just a small step and it's a simple idea, but don't let that fool you. It is extremely powerful.

Think back to the early days of your relationship, when things were going well and it was at its happiest.

Then ask yourself this question:

"What were some of the little things that I used to do that I know gave my spouse pleasure and made them feel loved and appreciated, but which I am no longer doing?"

The key is to think of *small* things. They might be a particular way you looked at them, a smile you gave them, something you would say to them, or a way in which you touched them.

Recall a time when your spouse seemed very happy to be with you. What were you doing, *specifically*, in that situation? What caused them to respond positively to you?

Once you have come up with one or two things - go and do them with your spouse again. Not in a big or dramatic way. Just casually do it and see what happens. It doesn't really matter where your marriage is right now.

Just make a small gesture, a small positive action and see what happens.

Don't have any expectations. Don't be concerned about how your spouse might react.

Just take one small step in the right direction of healing your marriage.

For you to change the direction of your marriage - for you to restore the love that you once had - you need to think and act differently. This exercise is a start in doing that.

A wonderfully fulfilling and happy marriage is possible for you. It's what you signed up for in the first place!

You're on your way...

Chapter 2: Uncounseling: The Key to Healing Your Relationship and Bringing Back Love

The first thing that most people think of if their marriage is in trouble, particularly if it's in a lot of trouble, is the 'need' for counseling. It is also what many other people would recommend as well.

So what is 'Uncounseling'?

Well it certainly is *not* an attack on counseling per se. Uncounseling is simply an approach to healing and restoring love that doesn't involve talking about and working on problems (which is what most counseling does).

The reality is that for many people, counseling isn't effective. The same is true for talking about the marriage and working on the problems with your spouse.

Sadly, because of the belief that counseling and focusing on the problems is the only answer, many marriages have ended when they need not have. This is obviously tragic.

Many people try counseling and find it ineffective or even counterproductive. Many others are unable to get their spouse to go to counseling in the first place. In both these instances they may mistakenly believe there are no other options for them and they simply give up on their marriage.

The truth is that it doesn't need to be that way. There is an alternative: Uncounseling.

The Truth About Counseling

Let's first look at counseling - and in particular marriage counseling - and at the reasons why it is so often not effective.

Before we begin, I should say that there are of course many, many well-meaning and highly skilled people offering counseling services. But the reality is that the success rate for marriage counseling is not high.

To understand why this is so, let's relate it to your own situation.

Here are some of the reasons why counseling probably wouldn't work for you and why it may well be detrimental to your relationship.

1. **You have already tried counseling and found it didn't work.**

   If that's the case, it seems illogical to repeat something that didn't have a positive effect or that may have made things worse.

2. **Lack of time.**

   This could be for several reasons (such as career, family or other commitments). And if your marriage is in a state where you're on the verge of splitting up, you might not have the luxury of spending weeks or months in counseling to try to resolve things.

3. Cost.

Counseling can be expensive. Counselors obviously charge for their time, and virtually all of them are going to tell you that you're going to need at least a few sessions before you will begin to see any results. The cost can add up quickly.

You might also attend more sessions than you intended to initially.

There is also a cost attached to your own time. You might need to take time off work, or at the very least you will not be able to be financially productive during the times you are with the counselor.

Of course, counseling is still much cheaper than a divorce if you consider the legal fees, the loss of your assets and all the additional expenses that are part of even a 'simple' divorce. Counseling looks like a cheap option!

Nevertheless, there is a cost involved and that might be something that you're not prepared or able to outlay, particularly if you feel that there is little chance of it being successful.

4. Your spouse may be resistant to attending counseling.

If your spouse does not want to heal your marriage and if they do in fact want to leave, there's probably not a lot you can do to get them to commit to serious counseling.

Even if you could persuade your spouse to go to counseling with you, it is unlikely that they will be prepared to do much if anything about healing your marriage if they simply don't want to.

The 'Problem' with Marriage Counseling

Although the above are reasons why counseling would not work for you, there are more fundamental reasons why marriage counseling in general has such a high failure rate.

Again, this is not meant as a criticism of the skills and intentions of the many wonderful people in the counseling profession.

However, there is no benefit in me not being honest with you. I have reached the conclusions I share with you here as a result of my own observations and experiences, as well as from other anecdotal and statistical sources.

Here are the main reasons I have identified as to why counseling is not generally effective for many marriages:

1. Imbalance of commitment.

Successful counseling generally relies on both spouses being equally willing and committed to go through the process. In reality, this usually isn't the case.

Even if both parties agree to counseling, that doesn't necessarily mean that they're equally willing and committed.

Most often, it is one spouse who suggests counseling and 'persuades' the other to take part.

Success also usually depends on the husband and wife remaining equally committed throughout the counseling process. This is far from guaranteed.

2. Not getting along with the counselor.

It often happens that when a couple gets into the counseling situation, one or the other doesn't particularly like the counselor or connect with them especially well.

It is not uncommon for one spouse to feel that they're being 'picked on' - that they're being focused on unfairly and/or pressured.

3. Third party limitations.

Marriage counseling generally requires two people to attempt to explain their situation - as they each see it - to a third person (the counselor).

The counselor will then interpret what they think is happening, and provide advice based on that.

The problem with that is that no one can ever understand a person's situation anywhere near as well as the person themselves. A counselor may attempt to help a person to reach their own 'right' conclusions and decisions but inevitably the counselor's own perspective will have an influence.

When trying to explain anything to another person, there is always the potential for miscommunication. And because of that, there is the risk of getting the wrong advice.

The only way to overcome this is for each person to explain their situation perfectly. Obviously, that is impossible to do.

4. Shift of responsibility.

Counseling has the tendency to take some of the responsibility for solving the problems away from the individuals themselves and put it on to the counselor. In other words, they may rely on the counselor to come up with the right answers for them.

When a person looks to someone else for advice on what to do about a problem, the person they are asking never knows them or their situation as well as they do.

Because of this, they are never going to be able to give the best possible advice. The solution must come from within the person with the problem themselves.

5. Focus is on the problems.

Counseling tends to focus on your problems and trying to find effective solutions for them.

However, one of the essential truths of life (and one of the guiding concepts of Uncounseling) is:

Whatever you focus on, you get more of.

If you focus on problems, that is what you will get more of.

Remember, problems are merely the symptoms of what's really going on in a situation.

Problems are not the real cause of things going wrong in your marriage - they are the result.

Even if you 'paper over the cracks' and manage to find answers to some of your problems, you're not going to achieve a permanent solution because you're not dealing with *why* these problems are occurring. You're not addressing the root cause.

The other thing about problems - and why it doesn't work to focus on trying to solve them - is that if you want to solve a problem, what that usually requires is that you and your spouse (either one or both of you) must *behave* differently.

But you can't change a behavior, at least in the long term, if you're not dealing with the underlying *cause* of the behavior. And you won't find that cause within the problem itself.

This concept will become clearer later in this book.

6. The nature of relationships in modern society.

The final reason why I believe the statistics have proven that counseling is just not effective anymore is that society today (and the role of relationships within that) is too complex for a 'cookie cutter' approach to work.

The "If X happens, do Y" approach of counseling comes from the belief that a single solution can be made to work for multiple situations. Perhaps it might have in our grandparents' day, but today it simply won't.

Relationships are much more complex than they used to be. The expectations we have for our marriages now are much higher than our grandparents had. Marriage is no longer just about children and survival.

We expect a marriage to bring us fulfilment, happiness and joy - in other words, to meet our emotional as well as physical needs.

Not only are modern relationships more complex, but the society we live in is itself much more complex than in earlier times.

We're all suffering from information overload. Just getting through the day seems to take enormous effort because of the huge amount of information that we are constantly being bombarded with.

Piling yet more information into your brain in the hope of healing your marriage is unlikely to be effective in achieving the desired results.

These are the main reasons why counseling is often not an effective solution for marriage problems.

And as I stated earlier, this isn't to negate the efforts of counselors or to say anything against them as people. Many are wonderful people who are highly skilled and have the best of intentions.

In some cases they may get a good result. But to create a happy, fulfilling marriage and even rescue it from divorce, counseling often is not going to be the real answer.

The Alternative to Marriage Counseling

There is an alternative to marriage counseling. I call it *Un*counseling because it takes a somewhat opposite - and counterintuitive - approach to that of most traditional counseling.

When you entered into your marriage or relationship, I'm sure that one of the words foremost in your mind was 'commitment'.

You agreed verbally - and even in writing - that you were committed to the marriage and whatever it entailed.

But what were you actually committing to? To be loving? To be faithful? To 'be there through thick and thin'? To 'make it work'?

While you may feel that you were and are committed to these things, this isn't particularly helpful when you are experiencing 'rough patches' in your relationship.

Being loving, faithful and determined sound like admirable qualities, but if you rely on these to heal your marriage you will ultimately fail.

This is for two reasons:

1. They are too vague.

> What does being loving, faithful and determined actually mean? These are states of mind, but they don't imply any action, even though it is only through your actions that you achieve results.

2. They don't account for your spouse's point of view.

> What if your spouse wants to end your marriage or doesn't want to change? Telling them and demonstrating that you love them and are committed to your marriage will probably not go down well with them.
>
> It will likely be seen as stubbornness, even stupidity and a disregard for their feelings.
>
> This won't make your spouse feel any better about you, and it will probably push the two of you even further apart.

So yes, you need to be committed - but not to your marriage. Instead, you need to be committed to building and maintaining what it is that enriches and strengthens your marriage: the **foundations** on which your marriage is built.

A lack of attention to the foundations of a marriage is at the core of all problems, unhappiness and the ending of relationships.

With strong foundations, your marriage can withstand any storm that comes your way. And upon them you can build any mighty structure that you desire.

This is what Uncounseling is all about.

Uncounseling is effective for anyone in any relationship or marriage, no matter what the 'problems' appear to be.

Now, that's a big claim to make.

However, the reason I can say that, and with a degree of confidence, is because Uncounseling doesn't rely on your spouse for it to work.

It doesn't depend on the skill of a counselor or therapist.

It doesn't rely on anyone or anything 'out there', or beyond your control.

In fact, Uncounseling works exactly because it focuses solely on the one thing that you have complete and total control over.

And that 'thing' is:

Yourself.

Uncounseling is **all** about **you**. And that's because of another fundamental truth about you and your marriage:

__The relationship that you have with your spouse is a reflection of the relationship that you have with yourself.__

This is a very powerful concept, and it is worth spending some time pondering over it. In fact, the more you do think about it, the more you will realize it's true.

> Counseling focuses on your marriage and your problems.
> Uncounseling focuses on **you**.

You cannot change your marriage.

You cannot change your spouse.

You can only change **you**.

Incidentally, if you've already tried to change your spouse, or any other person for that matter, you will already know that it doesn't work.

You may influence someone else, but you can never force them to change. They are the only one who can make changes to themselves.

The only person you are going to have any success in changing is **yourself**. And that's great news because **you** are the one and only person in your life who you do have total control over.

The Six Foundations of Uncounseling

Foundation #1: Understanding Who You Really Are

"Know Thyself"

These two words, attributed to Plato, were inscribed at the entrance of the Temple of Apollo in Delphi, Greece. They are probably the two most powerful words ever written.

The wisest philosophers and teachers throughout history have taught that knowing and understanding yourself is the key to your happiness and fulfilment (which is your life's purpose). And it's the key to your marriage happiness as well.

Make it your mission to get to know and understand the most important person in your life.

This person is more important than your spouse. They are more important than your children or anyone else you love or care about.

This person is **You.**

You can never fix anything in your life (including your marriage) by trying to fix it.

You can only fix something by fixing *yourself*.

And you can only fix yourself if you know who you are.

You are the cause of *everything* that happens to you in your life.

You might find it difficult to accept this statement. But by the time you have completed this book you will know it to be true.

How well do you know yourself?

Learning about yourself is a lifelong process - and your efforts will reward you in ways you can't imagine. Begin by answering the following questions:

- What drives you?
- What makes you do the things that you do?
- What's important to you?
- What are your strengths?
- What are your weaknesses?
- What makes you happy?
- What stops you from achieving success and happiness?

You will be diving into a lot more depth in this book to learn about the wonderful and fascinating person that you are.

Because the more you understand yourself, the better your life becomes.

Foundation #2: Knowing What You Really Want

If you don't know what you want in your life, it's unlikely that you will ever get it.

Very few people know what they **really** want.

- What do you want to have and do in your life?
- What do you want in your marriage?

You only get one life. As far as we know anyway. You might as well make the most of it - and knowing what you want is one of the keys to doing that.

Foundation #3: Understanding Your Spouse

You are not responsible for your spouse and their happiness. However, you can (and should) play a vital role in helping them achieve happiness for themselves.

But you can't do that unless you understand them and know what they want.

- What drives them and makes them happy?

- What do they want in their life?

- What do they want in a marriage?

We will be looking at these and other questions in much more detail in this book.

Foundation #4: Being Attractive

There is only one reason why your spouse wouldn't want to be with you and give you what you want and need to be happy. And that reason is very simple: **they don't feel good about you.**

And what's another way of saying 'not feeling good about you'?

They don't find you **attractive**.

The simplest and fastest way to get your marriage back on track is to make your spouse feel attracted to you. If you do that, they're going to want to stay with you. If they've already left, they're going to want to come back to you.

Think back to the early days of your relationship, to the time when you both were very attracted to each other. Did problems seem less significant or even nonexistent?

Of course. Even though there may have been problems, you hardly noticed them because you were focused on the positive aspects in your relationship.

Attractiveness is such a vital part of any marriage that there is an entire chapter devoted to this subject coming up (Chapter 5).

Foundation #5: Being an Effective Communicator

I am sure you would agree that open and honest communication is a vital part of any marriage. It is also one of the first things that 'goes' when a marriage encounters problems.

But for your marriage to be strong, the communication needs to be more than just open and honest. It needs to be **effective**.

By effective, I mean that your communication must create the desired result - which is to contribute to the happiness and wellbeing of both you and your spouse.

Building this Foundation of Uncounseling is the subject of Chapter 6.

Foundation #6: Being Fearless

It is only when you are fearless that you are truly free. When you have no fear, you feel confident, unshakeable and certain that you can achieve exactly what you want in your marriage and in your life.

You take the right actions that give you the right results. You become free to love unconditionally - yourself and others.

In contrast, feeling worried and afraid prevents you from seeing the truth about yourself. It stops you from taking the actions necessary to create your ideal marriage - and life.

In the last chapter of this book (Chapter 9) I will share with you a very powerful process for identifying and eliminating your fears.

When you are in a marriage without fears, the real magic happens!

Building and Strengthening the Six Foundations

As I have said in Foundation #1, the solutions to your marriage problems are all about you. Success comes from you working on yourself and yourself alone.

As such, you must take responsibility for **all** of your results in your life.

You must be prepared to accept:

"The situation I'm in now is of my own doing. I created it, I'm responsible for it, and I alone have the power to change it."

Now, your first reaction to this might be:

"It's not all my fault. My spouse should share some of the blame. I've been doing my best, but they haven't. I have changed, but they haven't. It's not fair to put it all on me!"

These statements may seem justified to you, but they're not going to help you. If you really want to heal your marriage and create the great relationship that you say you do, then you must cast all those thoughts aside.

Instead, realize that **you alone are responsible for your life, and for your life situation, and you - and you alone - have the power to create what you want.**

This is the opposite to what nearly everyone thinks. Throughout our lives we are fed the idea that we are not in control of our life.

The government, the economy, our employer, other people, and of course our spouse - all of these dictate to us how our life turns out. And we have little, if any, control over any of these.

Or so we have been led to think.

Most people believe these things. But most people aren't achieving the results they want in their life either. And they are not happy!

If you follow through with the exercises and ideas in this book - which are all about you and no-one else - you will be amazed at what happens.

And you will know with certainty that the truth is:

Your life - including your marriage - really is *all* up to you. When <u>you</u> change, your life changes.

Make the 6 Foundations of Uncounseling the foundations of your marriage and your life - and the changes you witness will be profound.

Chapter 3: Three Questions You Must Answer Before You Attempt to Heal Your Marriage

When people are confronted by problems in their marriage, usually their first and only response is to focus on trying to fix those problems.

Unfortunately, what they usually notice is that the path to healing their marriage by doing this is paved with stress, struggle, uncertainty and conflict.

And often things only seem to get worse.

This is because, as discussed in Chapter 1, a problem is merely a **symptom**. For a permanent solution you need to find and work on the **cause** - which is something that is not right in the structure (the foundations) of your marriage.

Very few people realize this, which is why the conflicts and hurts remain in so many marriages, no matter how much effort one or both spouses put in.

However, before you begin to address healing your marriage, there are three very important questions that you must answer.

Your answers to these questions will give you clarity on where you currently are in your marriage situation.

And they will help ensure that you move in the right direction so that you achieve the results that are best for you.

Question #1 "Is it actually <u>possible</u> to heal <u>my</u> marriage?"

This is often the first question I am asked by people struggling with their marriage.

It is very important to know the answer to this before you do anything else. After all, there is no point attempting to heal your marriage if the task is futile.

Your situation may look grim. Perhaps your spouse has told you that the marriage is over and cannot be healed. They might even have left already. The feelings between you might be filled with hostility, anger or indifference.

You might also be thinking that you have tried everything possible. You may have tried counseling. You may have spent hours talking with your spouse about how you can get your marriage working again. You may have read books or even taken courses.

Sadly, many people in this situation reach a place of despair, feeling that they just don't know what else to do. And what is even worse, they might accept that they can't heal their marriage.

They feel they must resign themselves to the fact that an unhappy relationship - or even a divorce - is inevitable.

If you are in that place where you have given up hope, you will agree that it's not a good place to be. At that point you may well be thinking:

"I have tried so many things and nothing has worked; maybe I should just give up".

Now, here's some good news.

If you are asking yourself, *"Can my marriage be healed?"* then the truth is:

If there is just *one* of you - either you or your spouse - who genuinely wants to heal the marriage, then it can be done.

It doesn't require both of you to want it (or think you want it).

It does require commitment - but that commitment need only come from one of you.

I am assuming that you are reading this because you are the person who does want to heal your marriage. So, the good news is you really can if you truly are willing.

This is true, even if you think you have already tried 'everything'. Incidentally, it's a certainty that you haven't tried 'everything'. In fact, with all due respect, I'd be willing to bet that you haven't tried much at all.

You may have put in a lot of effort, but you haven't tried many **different** things.

What are one hundred different things that you have tried to heal your marriage? How about fifty different things? Twenty? Ten?

If you can think of ten, then you're doing well - but it's a long way off 'everything'.

I am not saying this to make you feel bad, or to put you down in any way.

But what I am saying is: there **is** a solution to every problem. And your unhappy marriage is just a problem - so there must be a solution.

You just need to be motivated enough to keep going until you find the right solutions.

So, the question really is not, *"Can my marriage be healed?"*

The real question is:

"How motivated am I to heal it?"

If you are truly motivated, you will simply keep going until you find the right solutions.

Think carefully about this question and answer it honestly for yourself.

And then move on the second question, which is...

Question #2: "Is this the *right* marriage for me?"

Now that you know that your marriage *can* be healed - if you are motivated enough to find and apply the right information until you get the result - there is something even more important for you to realize.

In fact, this is not only important, it is vital:

If you are *not* in the *right* relationship, no matter how committed you are, you are *not* going to heal it.

A great cathedral can never be built out of straw on swampy

ground, no matter how much time and energy is spent on it. And you can never create a great marriage without the right foundations, built out of the right materials.

"Is this the *right* marriage for me?"

Are you and your spouse (still) suited to each other? Is your marriage able to provide you with what you really want and need?

I know that this is not easy to answer. However, it is vitally important than you do - and answer honestly and correctly. There is nothing worse than struggling on for years trying to fix the problems in your marriage if the reality is that you and your spouse are simply not compatible.

In that situation you will never solve all your problems - more will keep showing up. And no matter how hard you try, true happiness will elude you.

On the other hand, it would be tragic to end your marriage, thinking that you and your spouse are no longer right for each other, if all you needed was to do a few things in a slightly different way to get all the happiness you wanted.

So answer this question very carefully. And to help you arrive at the right conclusion, here are a number of further questions and things to consider.....

The Importance of the *Right* Marriage

Firstly, let us examine *why* it's important to be in the right marriage or relationship. This comes down to answering one of the biggest questions in this book which is:

What is the true purpose of your life?

This is something that every philosopher, thinker and religious teacher throughout history has asked themselves.

Many books have been written in an attempt to answer this question. You yourself may have asked this at times as well.

Although it might appear on the surface to be a difficult and complicated question, the truth is that the real answer is surprisingly simple.

And it is the single answer that all science, religion, spirituality and philosophy agree on.

Here's a story that will explain what this answer is....

* * *

There was once a man who was shipwrecked on a remote island. He was washed up on a beach and in a sorry state.

He was found by some local tribespeople who took him back to their village and nursed him back to health. Thanks to their kindness, he gradually regained his strength and soon he settled into village life.

As time went on, the man began to be aware that, for the first time in his life, he felt truly happy. He had lived as a businessman in a big city, rich and successful but with a great deal of pressure and stress.

Here, however, he felt no stress.

Life in the village was very simple. The days were spent fishing and looking after the village. At night everyone would eat a meal together before gathering around the fire to share stories, songs and games.

And as he worked and lived amongst the tribe, the man sensed in himself a true joy and happiness that he had never felt before.

One evening, as he was sitting by the fire and enjoying the happy scene around him, he turned to one of the elders who was sitting next to him and asked:

"O wise one, what do you think the true purpose of life is?"

The other villagers, overhearing his words, fell silent. They all looked at him with friendly yet puzzled stares. The elder smiled at him and said quietly:

"Don't you know? The purpose of life is to be happy."

* * *

Is there really any other purpose to life than to be happy?

Anyone who has seriously studied this question has come to the conclusion that there isn't. Biologically, emotionally, culturally, spiritually - our whole purpose for being alive is to be happy.

Your marriage plays a vital role in your happiness. It's there to help you to be happy. But your marriage will only do that if it meets your needs and helps to bring out the best in you as a human being.

Your marriage won't do that if it causes you to continue to struggle and feel stressed and anxious.

It's obvious that if you're not in the right marriage, then you're not going to be happy. And not only that, but you're not going to be able really to give of your best - both to other people and to yourself - or to live to your full potential. Your life will be more difficult than it should be, and you will never experience the fullness of what true love - and life - is.

The other thing you need to bear in mind is that if you are not in the right marriage then you're going to be sending out the wrong messages to those who you care about - such as your children - about what a marriage really is and should be.

You should endeavor to live to your highest potential because that is the example you want to set - for others and for yourself.

So, it's not just important to be in the right marriage, it's vital.

Stay or Go? How Do You Know?

Let's look more closely at Question #2:

"Is this the *right* marriage for me?"

Unfortunately, this question becomes even more difficult to answer when you are having marriage problems. That's because emotional stress creates doubt and confusion in the mind.

Your judgement becomes clouded, even though it is more important than ever that you make sensible and rational decisions for your marriage and your life.

Here is a six-step process that will help you to become clear about whether your marriage is the right one for you or not.

Step #1: Know what you really want and need to be happy

This is of course the second Foundation of Uncounseling.

Remember, being happy is not just what you want, it's your life purpose.

What is it specifically that will give **you** true happiness?

I'm not only referring here to material things such as an amount of money, what sort of car you want to drive or the holidays you want to take.

What you really need to know is, what are the **feelings** that you **need** for you to be happy? How do you want to **feel** on a day-by-day and moment-by-moment basis?

Here are some further questions that will help you to clarify this.

1. What feelings are important to you?

Everyone has different sorts of feelings that are important to them. What are the most important feelings to you?

For example, they could be: peace, security, freedom, adventure, love, intimacy, passion.

Which of these (and others) would you most like to experience?

2. What do you want to achieve in your life?

When you are on your death bed, what do you want to remember about your life? What do you want others to say about you after you have gone? What do you want your life to have meant in the eyes of other people as well as to yourself?

3. What are three activities that make you truly happy?

What are three things that you do currently (or that you could do) that make you happy?

Are they humorous situations? Are they dangerous situations? Are they where you're learning new things? Are they activities where you feel calm, relaxed and safe?

4. What is your ideal lifestyle?

In your ideal world, how would you want to live?

For instance, would you like to live peacefully in the countryside on a piece of land with a few animals and a simple lifestyle? Or would you want to travel around the world on a wild adventure?

Would you want to go to Africa as a missionary? Would you want to run your own business? Would you prefer to stay at home and just look after your children?

Don't put any limitations on your imagination here. Don't say to yourself,

"This isn't realistic. I could never have or do that."

The purpose of this exercise is not to make this lifestyle a reality. It's merely to help you understand the sort of person that you are.

Step #2: Define your Ideal Marriage

Mentally step out of your current situation and imagine a 'theoretical world' in which you're living in your Ideal Marriage. It may or may not be with your current spouse.

Create a picture of how your life would look if you had a perfectly happy marriage.

What would you be **doing?** What would you be **feeling?**

Can you perhaps imagine the two of you backpacking around South America, staying at a different place every night? Or would the two of you be building a business together?

Would the two of you be living on a quiet farm somewhere in the countryside? Or living in a city with an exciting career and fast-paced lifestyle?

And how would you make each other feel? What feelings would you be giving to each other? Peace? Excitement? Security? Adventure?

In Chapter 4 we will be going into a lot more detail about what your perfect marriage would look like. For the purpose here, however, complete this exercise by making this picture as detailed as you can.

Step #3: Partner Match

'Partner Match' is where you take your answers from Steps #1 and #2 and apply them to your current situation.

Begin by answering the same questions in Steps #1 and #2, but this time about your spouse.

1. What feelings are important to *them*?
2. What do *they* want to achieve in their life?
3. What are three activities that make *them* truly happy?
4. What is *their* ideal lifestyle?
5. What would *their* Ideal Marriage look like?

If possible, get your spouse's help to answer these questions. Even better, have the two of you complete this exercise separately and come together with your answers.

However, if neither of these are possible (if your spouse is not available or willing), answer them on your own. The exercise will still be effective for you.

Now you have two sets of answers, one for yourself and the other for your spouse. And here comes the all-important question:

How do these lists compare?

How much overlap is there between what you and your spouse want and need for each of you to be happy?

Are you and your spouse wanting the same things? Do you want the same lifestyle? And most importantly, are you wanting the same feelings?

In simple terms, how compatible are the two of you?

From my experience, nearly all conflict in a relationship or a marriage (assuming that both people are mentally stable) is caused by a mismatch in desired feelings and desired lifestyle.

It is this mismatch that causes most of the communication conflicts, the lack of intimacy, the arguments and all the other problems.

There are two more questions to ask yourself in this step #3:

1. Are you truly willing and able to meet your spouse's needs?

You need to consider how different your spouse's needs and wants are from your own and whether you're actually happy to meet their needs.

If your needs are very different, would trying to meet your spouse's needs make you happy as well? If not, resentment is likely to build over time which will only be detrimental to your relationship.

2. Is your spouse truly able to meet your needs?

Do you honestly feel that your spouse could make you truly happy?

As always, you need to be very honest with yourself in answering these questions. Your happiness and - the happiness of others who you care about - depends on it.

Step #4: Identify *Why* You Got Married

Your aim here is to identify something that many people find very difficult to face:

Did you and your spouse get married for the *right* reasons?

In other words, did you get married because you thought you could truly make each other happy?

To answer this question, describe the story of the time from when you first met until the time you got married.

Recount everything that you can remember leading up to your marriage as if you were describing it to somebody else. Include significant events, what you were doing and, very importantly, what you were feeling.

When you have created your story, take a look at it and ask yourself:

"How much did we have in common during the time leading up to our marriage? Were we both looking for the same feelings and lifestyle? Did we share similar hopes and dreams?"

Then ask yourself:

"When we decided to get married, did I have any doubts, fears or uneasy feelings?"

This is different from simple 'marriage jitters'. It is a deep uneasiness, a sense of a 'little voice' saying to you: *"You shouldn't be doing this"* or *"It doesn't feel right".*

Did you have any thoughts such as:

- *"I won't find someone else better,"*
- *"It's better than being on my own,"*
- *"I feel like it's expected or that I must get married,"*
- *"The relationship isn't perfect, but it's good enough."*

All of the above reasons are based on fear — and they are not the best reasons. We'll have a lot more to say about fears (and the role they play in your marriage) later in this book.

Are things becoming clearer already? Perhaps the truth is already beginning to make itself obvious. Nevertheless there are two further steps....

Step #5: Identify your true feelings for your spouse right *now*

Over time, people change. You and your spouse are different people to who you were when you met. And your feelings will be different as well.

So even more important than knowing how you felt about your spouse when you got married is to know how you feel about them right now.

Here is a way to do that:

1. List all the things you *like* about your spouse.

> What do you admire about your spouse? What makes you smile when you think about them? What personal qualities do they have that impress you?
>
> They may (or may not) be things that were part of the initial attraction between the two of you.
>
> Include everything that you like and admire, including things about their personality, their viewpoints, attitudes and beliefs, their habits and their behaviors.

2. List all the things about your spouse that you *don't* like and would like to change.

> Many people in a troubled marriage find this a much easier list to write! List everything that irritates or upsets you about your spouse, including their habits, viewpoints, beliefs and behaviors.

Once you have your lists, take a look at the second one (what you don't like about your spouse) and answer the following:

1. How *important* is it to you that your spouse change what you don't like about them?

> Rate each item on your list on a scale of 1 to 10, 1 being *"It doesn't matter to me at all if they change this or not,"* to 10, being *"It's absolutely vital that they change this for me to keep my sanity!"*

2. How *difficult* would it be for your spouse to change what you don't like?

> For each item on your list, how difficult do you think it would be for them to change it?
>
> Again, rate each on a scale of 1 to 10, 1 being very easy for them to change and 10 being it would probably be something impossible for them to change.

These two questions help you to see how you really feel about your spouse right now. It is also a reality check on how compatible you are as well.

Here is the last step. It's a big wakeup call for many people and I want you to think carefully about it....

Step #6: Identify Why You Are In Your Marriage Right Now

Why are you *still* in your marriage? Even if you are not facing major problems, it's important to know the real reasons why you are committing to this marriage.

There will be two types of reasons: positive reasons and negative reasons.

1. What are the *positive* reasons why you are in your marriage?

> Think about the good reasons why you want to hold onto your marriage and why you want it to work. It may be because you remember the good times with your spouse, and you want to relive those.

You may also recognize the good qualities that your spouse has, the things about them you really love and admire. Or you may see how much the two of you have in common and the great things that you could do and achieve together.

2. What are the *negative* reasons why you are in your marriage?

This is the flip side of the coin. You will find that most if not all of these reasons are based on some sort of **fear**.

Many people unfortunately only stay in a marriage or in a relationship that's not right for them because of their fears. This is a very big topic in itself and we will cover it in detail in the final chapter. But for the purpose of this process, identify any fears that you have that are keeping you in your marriage.

Some common fears are:

- Guilt: the guilt you think you would feel if the marriage ended.

- Shame: the worry of what your family, friends or even your children might think of you if your marriage didn't succeed.

- Finances: a divorce may make things difficult for you financially.

- Uncertainty: you may not know where else to go or what to do to move on with your life.

- Impact on your children: You might be thinking:
  "I don't want my children to be brought up in a broken home, so for their sake I'm staying."

- Cultural or religious reasons: It may be against your cultural or religious beliefs to end your marriage.
- Loneliness: a fear of being alone and not being loved.

Identify as many reasons as you can think of as to why you're still holding onto your marriage. Make sure you uncover both positive and negative ones.

* * *

If you have given yourself some time to consider and answer these questions - and have been honest with yourself - you should have a clear picture of whether or not your marriage is the right one for you. You should have an indication if the relationship is able to give you what you need to be truly happy in your life.

Of course, knowing the answer is one thing and what you do with this knowledge is another. However, with this clarity it will be much easier for you to move ahead in the right direction.

Remember, the purpose of your life is to be happy! The purpose of your marriage is to contribute to that.

Don't feel guilty about wanting to be happy. When you are happy, you are being the 'real you' - and can give the best to yourself and to others.

It is what you are here to be.

Question #3: "What do I need to <u>do</u> to heal my marriage?"

Arriving at the right answer for Question #2 *("Is this the <u>right</u> marriage for me?")* can take considerable effort. This is why I have gone into such detail about it.

But it is vitally important - in fact, it's amongst the most important questions to 'get right' in this entire book.

Once you know that you **can** heal your marriage and that it's the **right** marriage for you, then all it comes down to is identifying - and doing - the things that will give you the right result.

A key to answering this third question is to understand what creates real change in people and relationships. After all, change is what you want.

Change comes about, not through logic or common sense, but through *emotions and feelings.*

If you want change in your marriage, you must do the things that change the *feelings* that are taking place in your marriage.

Most people, most of the time, never use this approach when dealing with the issues in their marriage. Instead, they try to 'figure things out' and force change by using logic.

But the truth is, people don't behave in a logical way. They behave the way they do because of how they *feel.*

You and your spouse may be being hostile towards each other and having frequent arguments. You may even have stopped talking.

However, none of these behaviors will help your marriage. They don't make you feel any better about each other.

It doesn't make logical sense for you or your spouse to act this way either. But you're doing these things anyway because your behavior is driven by your feelings rather than by common sense.

People almost always behave the way they do for the feelings they get, not for logical reasons. This is a characteristic of being human. And it can cause people to do things that appear to be irrational and even 'crazy'.

This is why you hear stories of a multimillionaire's wife who has run off with gardener. Or why a successful businessman has left his wife for his secretary. Or why someone has an affair, even while knowing that if they are discovered it could mean the end of their marriage.

These behaviors don't make any logical sense. A person does not leave their 'suitable' spouse for someone 'unsuitable', because it will make their life more comfortable physically (money, etc.). They do not have an affair to end their marriage.

They do it because in the new relationship they are getting (or think they will get) their emotional needs met. The 'other' person makes them feel good, no matter how unsuitable they may appear from a logical perspective.

If you use logic to try to heal your marriage you are going to fail. You can't say to your spouse:

"Look at all of the nice things I do for you. Look at the great lifestyle we have. You should be happy in our marriage!"

Feelings almost always override logic when it comes to the actions and behaviors of humans.

The simple reason why your marriage is struggling is that you and your spouse are no longer meeting each other's *emotional needs*.

You are no longer giving each other the *feelings* that you both want.

Usually one person is more strongly motivated to end the marriage than the other, and they are the one whose emotional needs are being met even less.

So, if you think your spouse wants to leave you or is not as involved in your marriage as you would like, rather than blaming them or being resentful, think about their emotional needs. Are they being met in your marriage?

* * *

What I am getting at is this: If you really want to heal your marriage, what you must **do** is to focus on the **emotional** states (the feelings) that are being generated between you and your spouse.

You can certainly affect your spouse's emotions. You know this because at the moment, the way you are behaving is probably causing them to have negative feelings towards you.

But it is within your power to change that - you just need to know how.

I once met a man who was in the final stages of planning to separate. He and his wife were heading for divorce.

It was a sad situation, but he made an interesting comment. He said that his wife had told him that she used to love him, but now everything he did irritated her.

In other words, his behaviors were causing his wife to have negative **feelings**. Being around him did not make her **feel** good.

Imagine if this man could have found a way (or ways) to make his wife feel good when she was around him? That would be all it would have taken to save that marriage.

So stop your spouse's negative feelings towards you.

Replace them with positive feelings.

If your spouse feels good around you, there is no way they are ever going to want to leave. And they will not only want to stay - but they will also want to contribute to making your marriage better.

And if they have already left, they are going to want to come back. And it won't take long!

You are probably thinking at this point:

*"Can this actually be done? Can I really have such an influence on **my** spouse?"*

You certainly can. Psychology has proven that we have the power to change the way others think and feel. And if you don't believe this, just look at the advertising industry.

Advertisers use specific tools and techniques to get you to feel good about their product with the sole aim of getting you to buy it. Advertisers really know how to influence human behavior by affecting the way people feel.

In a similar way, politicians and even religious leaders also use emotion to attract and motivate their followers to commit to their cause. In extreme cases, people will even sacrifice their life for a cause or for their beliefs. They don't do this for logical reasons - but for the feelings they get (of glory, heroism, importance and so on).

You also use the same tools and techniques of 'emotional influence' in your interactions with other people (including your spouse). You are just not usually aware of it.

At the moment you're probably doing a skillful job of creating negative feelings in your spouse and pushing them away from you.

Wouldn't it be great if you could consciously make your spouse feel *good* around you? I am not talking here about using mind control, manipulating them or trying to get them to do anything they don't want to do.

It's simply about finding ways to help them to feel good rather than to feel bad.

So the answer to this third question:

"What do I need to do to heal my marriage?"

is....

You need to change the *emotional state* of your marriage from negative to positive.

How to do that forms the basis for Uncounseling, and the rest of this book.

* * *

If your conclusion is to leave your marriage...

Have you worked through all of the exercises in this chapter and reached the honest conclusion that your marriage is not right for you?

If that is the case, I would like to encourage you to act on that conclusion. Your happiness is the most important thing.

However, also work through the rest of this book. It may be that your conclusion is not correct and that, with the additional ideas and information provided here, you come to see your marriage is in fact right for you.

At the very least, this book will give you the ideas and skills you need to make any relationship you may have in the future a success.

Chapter 4: What Sort of Marriage Do You Want?

You will recall that Uncounseling Foundation #2 is: Knowing what you really want.

This is in fact one of the fundamental principles of success in anything: You must know what you want.

Whether it be in your finances, career or health, you won't make much progress if you don't have a clear goal or picture of what you are trying to achieve.

In this chapter you will get clear on exactly what you want for your marriage. This will give you a 'target to shoot at'. Creating a successful marriage will then become simply a question of following the right steps to get there.

The Perfect Marriage?

What would a 'perfect marriage' look like for you?

This is one of the first things I often ask when coaching someone who is unhappy with their marriage. The response I get back is usually a puzzled look or blank stare.

Very few people have ever stopped to think about what they really want in their marriage, beyond being 'happy'. People are so bound up in their problems that it has never occurred to then to consider very carefully what their ideal marriage would actually look like.

But this is a critically important question to answer. If you don't know what you're looking for, then the chances are slim to none that you're going to find it.

Before we uncover the answer for you and your marriage, let's examine why it is that this question is so overlooked.

The main reason is because most people simply don't **believe** that a perfect marriage is possible.

If you don't **believe** that you can have a perfect marriage, you will continue to think and do the things that prevent you from having it. You get you what you believe in.

The beliefs and expectations that give you a marriage you **don't** want (rather than the marriage you **do** want) are not only unhelpful, but they are usually completely incorrect.

Most of what you believe or expect about marriage has been given to you by the culture in which you live, and you've been brought up to accept that these things are true.

If you look at the state of most marriages today, you will have to conclude that whatever most people have been taught to believe about marriage is leading them down the wrong track.

Here are some of the most common false ideas that most people have been conditioned to believe are true, and which prevent them from having their own perfect marriage.

False Marriage Belief #1: "All marriages have problems"

A relationship simply does *not* have to have problems.

Did *you* have problems in your relationship in the early days when you and your spouse got together?

I'd venture to suggest that you probably didn't or, if there were 'problems', that they were trivial and not important to you.

In addition, what some people would call a problem other people call a challenge. This is a powerful distinction that will ensure you deal with 'issues' in a much more constructive way.

And this isn't just playing with words. It's an entirely different approach that creates completely different results.

> Problems are something you struggle with, with a negative mindset.
> Challenges are something you deal with, with a positive mindset.

Whichever mindset you choose – and it is a choice - will make all the difference to the results you get. With a positive mindset, you may even look forward to your 'challenges' because you know that dealing with them will be of benefit to your life (more about this in a later chapter).

False Marriage Belief #2: "A successful marriage takes hard work"

We're led to believe that marriage requires struggle and doing things that are difficult, tiring and unpleasant. This holds so many relationships back and, again, it's simply not true.

Think of something that you love to do, perhaps a hobby or interest. When you are involved in the activity, do you find it difficult, tiring and unpleasant?

Sometimes it may involve doing new things or overcoming challenges. But overall, isn't it true that you wouldn't describe your hobby as hard work? You do it because you enjoy it. And doing what you enjoy doesn't seem like hard work at all.

Your hobby or pleasurable activity requires some effort. But it's enjoyable effort.

It's the same thing with a marriage. If you're enjoying being in your marriage, you don't see it as hard work.

False Marriage Belief #3: "My marriage can never be perfect"

This belief is the source of all of the reasons and excuses you give for why you're not happy in your relationship. You might say things such as:

"We're too different from each other."

"My spouse has changed (or I have changed) and they're not the person they used to be."

"We just have too many problems for us to ever really be happy together."
"Our marriage is not perfect, but it is good enough."

You may feel that these are valid reasons for why your marriage is not as you would like.

But this belief will hold you back from doing the things that can transform your relationship.

The Eight Components of the Perfect Marriage

Clearly, there are subtle yet big differences between people who have wonderful marriages and those who don't. But what is a **perfect** marriage?

There's a simple definition:

The perfect marriage is one in which your (and your spouse's) emotional needs are met.

This means that not only are you happy to be in your marriage - but that you experience true joy and fulfilment within it.

You would rather be in your marriage than anywhere else, or with anyone else or doing anything else. And your marriage allows you to be who you truly are, without fear or hurt.

When you understand that this is what a perfect marriage is, you also realize that it is attainable. And when you do, you can start taking the necessary steps to achieving it.

What does the perfect marriage look like in practice? What is really necessary for you to have your emotional needs met in your marriage?

There are eight components of the perfect marriage.

Component #1: The marriage comes first

In a perfect marriage, you and your spouse put your marriage first. It's your top priority. It's the reference point for everything else in your life.

That doesn't mean that you live in each other's pockets and that you don't do anything without the other. But you always consider the impact on your marriage of anything you do (or want to do).

You're willing to make sacrifices, although to you they're not actually sacrifices - because there is nothing better than being with your spouse.

Component #2: Commonality

The second element of a perfect marriage is that you and your spouse have a lot in common.

It is said that 'opposites attract' but when it comes to relationships, this is not true at all.

People in a great relationship have a lot in common. They have common interests. They do a lot of things together, things that they both passionately enjoy and are interested in.

They also have similar attitudes, values and beliefs. They tend to agree on most things, especially those that have the biggest impact on their life.

Component #3: Spending time together

This is a consequence of the previous two components. People in a perfect marriage spend a lot of time together. It is logical that you would spend a lot of time together if your marriage is your highest priority and you have a lot in common with your spouse.

You may hear people say in a marriage:

"We need to give each other space."

I certainly don't suggest that having time alone is going to have a negative effect on your marriage. But my observation is that 'giving each other space' is not a concept found in perfect marriages. People in such relationships literally don't feel the *need* to have space.

Certainly, sometimes they might want some time on their own, but there is not a burning desire or need to get away from each other.

Component #4: Loving the other for who they are, not who they would like them to be

This means not trying to change your spouse (which, as we have discussed earlier, is not possible anyway).

It means not saying (or thinking) things such as:

"If you would only do ____, I would love you more," or:

"I wish you wouldn't ____."

This is an important thing to consider in your own marriage.

Do you love your spouse for who they **are**, or do you have some picture of who you think they **could** or **should** be, and you wish they were that instead?

Do you feel you would love your spouse a lot more if they were somehow different in some of their behaviors or attitudes?

There is actually an expression for loving someone as they are:

Unconditional Love.

In a perfect marriage, a person's love for their spouse does not depend on what their spouse says or does.

Component #5: Allowing the other to make mistakes without letting it affect the marriage

How you and your spouse respond to each other's mistakes will be one of the main determinants of the quality of your marriage.

People in a perfect marriage understand that making mistakes is human. They don't take the mistakes of their spouse personally.

They allow their spouse to make mistakes without thinking that they are doing anything intentionally to harm their relationship. They don't see anything that their spouse does as a threat to their marriage.

Component #6: Totally open and effective communication

The quality of any relationship is based on the quality of the communication.

Totally open communication means the sharing of all thoughts, including fears, wants, desires, and even fantasies. Effective communication means having these thoughts heard and understood fully by the other person.

Can you tell your spouse absolutely anything without a fear of them being hurt or you being hurt?

Communication on that level is rare, but it's a mark of a perfect marriage.

Open and effective communication is of course one of the Foundations of Uncounseling. There is also an entire chapter coming up (Chapter 6) specifically about how to create this.

Component #7: Being in the relationship only by choice

The next important characteristic of a perfect marriage is that the two people are there for one reason and one reason only: they **want** to be there.

There is no sense of obligation or restriction. This means that they can (and they know they can and should) end their marriage at any time if their needs or their spouse's needs are not being met.

This allows them freedom in the marriage - the freedom to be themselves and to allow their spouse to be themselves.

This does not mean that either person has any intention of leaving the relationship. It does not mean they are not committed to the marriage.

They are committed to each other, and their intention is to stay, but they each know and accept that the purpose of their marriage is to meet their own and each other's emotional needs.

Their marriage is based on honesty. A person in a marriage is not being honest with their spouse or with themselves if they're staying in the relationship knowing that their (or their spouse's) emotional needs cannot be met.

Component #8: Having no fears for the marriage

Imagine being in a marriage where you weren't afraid of being hurt, you weren't afraid of hurting your spouse, you weren't afraid of making mistakes, you weren't afraid of them making mistakes, you weren't afraid of saying the wrong things or of them saying the wrong things - and you weren't afraid that your spouse might leave you or that the marriage might end.

You would be free to simply enjoy yourself - by being yourself. You would love yourself for who you are.

And you would do the same for your spouse. You would allow them to enjoy being themselves, and you would love them for who they are.

You may have fears in your marriage right now. However, by developing all the previous 7 components (which we will be doing throughout this book), you will eventually arrive at a place in your relationship where there is no fear.

This is a place that very few people get to in their marriage, but it's where all the magic happens.

It's an amazing place to be - and it's the perfect marriage.

How to Create Your Own Perfect Marriage

Perhaps from where you are right now, a perfect marriage sounds virtually impossible to attain.

You might be thinking:

*"This all sounds good in theory, but how could I possibly turn **my** marriage into something like this? It could never happen."*

However, it is very possible. All you need is:

1. Clarity on what you want
2. The right mindset (beliefs and attitudes)
3. The right actions

Use the eight Components above to get clear on what the perfect marriage would look like for you. Then use the rest of this book to integrate the right mindset and actions into your life.

By doing so, you can make your perfect marriage a reality.

Chapter 5: The Real Reason Why the Passion Goes - And How to Get it Back

One of the major causes of divorce and unhappiness in marriages is a lack of attraction. And there are few things that are worse than finding that you and your spouse no longer have romantic feelings for each other.

This chapter looks at the real reasons why attraction wanes in a relationship. You'll learn that it has nothing do to with the length of time you have been together, but everything to do with what you and your spouse are thinking and doing.

I then outline a step-by-step process to reignite the attraction in your marriage. This works because it deals with the 'attraction triggers' that are built into every person.

If your marriage is suffering from a lack of attraction, then this chapter is for you.

The Lack of Attraction Problem

Attraction is one of the important components of a loving relationship. However, it creates a real problem when it disappears or lessens over time.

One of the most saddening things that you will ever hear from your spouse is:

"I'm sorry, I'm just not attracted to you anymore."

This can be absolutely devastating, and not only will it leave you feeling hurt but probably also give you a sense of helplessness and thinking you just don't know what to do.

And after all, what **can** you do about somebody who's no longer attracted to you? What can you do if the passionate feelings are simply no longer there?

Perhaps you have already tried many times and in many ways to rekindle the passion and attraction, but nothing has worked.

In this chapter we are going to examine what attraction and passion really is. What creates it. What causes it to go away. And what can you do to get it back.

Firstly, some reassuring news. You **can** rebuild attraction and passion. It is within your control.

Despite what you might think, passionate attraction is not something mysterious which depends on chemistry, libido, how old you are or even what you look like (although appearance is important and we're going to discuss that shortly).

Because passion and attraction are not dependent on these 'mysterious' things, it also means that if you and your spouse have been passionately attracted to each other in the past (which presumably was the case) then you can get these feelings back.

What is Attraction - *Really*?

Before we get into the specifics of how to rebuild the passion and attraction between you and your spouse, let's talk a little bit about what attraction really is and why it is so important.

One of the problems in relationships today is that there are many myths and erroneous beliefs about attraction. This creates a great deal of confusion, pain and pressure, all of which put additional strains on a marriage.

Many, if not all, of these false ideas are created and fueled by the media.

Everywhere you look - in advertisements, magazines, movies and so on - you see examples of what 'passionate attraction' supposedly is. There are images and scenarios of people being lustfully attracted to each other, consumed by romantic joy and excitement.

Two people meet, instantly fall in love, and build a life together, filled with passion and bliss - and no problems.

But real life isn't like what's in the movies or the advertisements. This creates expectations in our society which are not only unrealistic, but impossible to attain.

So, if the common portrayal of attraction is based on myths, then what *is* passionate attraction in reality?

If you are like most people, when you hear the words 'passionate attraction', your first thought may be of lust and sizzling hot sex (just like in the movies!).

Sexual chemistry is certainly a key component of passionate attraction. As humans we are biological in nature. We are physical/biological entities that are 'programmed' to be sexual and to express our sexual energy in the form of attraction. It's how life works.

This is a wonderful thing. The dynamic that balances masculine and feminine is one of the most powerful energies in the universe.

And when you harness this energy within a loving, sexual, intimate relationship, you create one of the most beautiful things that you can experience.

So sexual energy is very important in attraction. It's what raises a relationship beyond and above just being a friendship.

And it connects us to our true inner nature, our spirit and the essence of who we are, because at our very heart we are sexual beings. It's the way we express our humanness.

However, passionate attraction is much more than physical sexual chemistry.

As a relationship develops, sexual attraction changes, and often diminishes.

You may have experienced this. What began as a very intense, fresh feeling transitions into a more solid, deeper form of attraction. This is the ideal. However, for most people, unfortunately, their relationship goes in the opposite direction and the attraction wanes.

So, there is a better definition of passionate attraction within a relationship. And that definition is:

Passionate Attraction is having your deepest emotional needs met.

In other words, passionate attraction occurs in a marriage relationship when each spouse feels **deeply loved**.

Love is a human's deepest emotional need. If you and your spouse make each other feel truly and deeply loved, you will feel intensely attracted to each other.

How do you make your spouse feel good emotionally - truly loved? How do you make them feel excited, safe, aroused, pleasured and happy (preferably all at the same time!)?

If you can make your spouse feel these things, they are going to feel attracted to you.

And if your spouse does the same for you - makes you feel good to be around them - then you are going to feel attracted to them as well.

Now all of this may seem rather obvious. But is it what is happening in your marriage?

If the passion and attraction has waned, then chances are that it isn't. We'll look at the real reasons why next.....

Why Passionate Attraction Diminishes

A major problem in most marriages, is that the attraction diminishes. But, despite the best of intentions, what causes this to happen?

What makes you feel less attracted to the person you fell in love with, married, and who at one time felt very passionate about?

You might think that the passage of time is the cause. That's certainly one of the major reasons most people would give. A common statement is:

"We've been together for a long time so it's natural that we should feel less attracted to each other."

However, time is not the primary reason. It cannot be because there are couples who are passionately attracted to each other after years of being together.

Another reason often given for waning attraction is that it is due to external pressures and stresses of life that are affecting the relationship.

These can include the demands created by the arrival of children.

Or there could be financial pressures. If you're working hard and struggling to pay the bills, that can have an effect (or appear to have an affect) on the level of passionate attraction experienced in your marriage.

Perhaps you may have other problems, such as health issues, career of business pressures or other difficulties.

Another thing I often hear is:

"I just have low libido. It's a medical/chemical/physical condition that means my sex drive is not what it was."

(Note: I am not a doctor. It is true that changes in the physical body can lead to a reduction in sex drive. If you believe this could be the case for you or your spouse, it would be worth investigating medically.)

All of these may appear to be the cause of a lack of attraction.

However, apart from in some medical cases, they're not actually the true cause.

The true cause is quite simple:

Passionate Attraction has gone because you and your spouse have stopped doing the things that make you feel passionately attracted to each other.

Of course, if you're under pressure and stressed by aspects of your life situation or if you've been together for a while and are just taking each other for granted, you are going to stop doing those things because they're going to seem to be less important or interesting to you.

You feel that you have higher priorities in your life than spending the time and energy on your marriage. But it doesn't get away from the truth that you have stopped doing the very things that created and sustained the attraction in the first place.

Here's a good example that will illustrate why this is true.

There are many people who have had an affair (or who are having one), who, while in the middle of experiencing the issues discussed above, don't feel passionately attracted to their spouse - but still manage to feel attracted to someone else.

A person can be having a passionate affair with someone while feeling low libido and low attraction for their own spouse. That shows very clearly that waning passionate attraction is not caused by time together, external pressures or physiological changes.

A person may be stressed and bored in their marriage, but still feel passionate attraction - it's just it's towards the wrong person!

So, the trick, if you want to get the attraction back, is to identify those things that created the attraction in the first place and start doing them again (and with your spouse, not someone else!).

How to Be Attractive to Your Spouse Again

Getting your spouse to feel passionately attracted to you comes down to two very basic things:

- You **being** an attractive person
- You **doing** attractive things

Attractiveness is one of the foundations of Uncounseling.

And it falls into three separate categories. They are: being **physically** attractive, creating an attractive **personality** and creating an attractive **marriage**.

#1: Being Physically Attractive

What happens when you've been with somebody for a while is that you tend to let your physical appearance deteriorate. The longer your relationship continues, the less effort you may make to please and impress your spouse with how you look.

Contrast this to what was happening when you and your spouse first got together. I'd be willing to bet that if you knew you were going out on a date with your spouse (or even before you'd ever met them), you'd have put in some effort to look nice.

You would have wanted to create a good impression, to make them feel good about you and to be attracted to you.

However, what happened after you'd been together for a while? You stopped wearing the nice clothes or being as well groomed.

So, to rebuild the attraction, your physical attractiveness is a good place to start. Here are some of the ways to do that.

1. Create an attractive body.

You don't need to look like Superman (or Woman). But if you're overweight, if you've lost your muscle tone, or if you're simply not looking or feeling good, do something to get back in shape. Exercise. Eat healthier foods and cut down on those foods and drink that harm your body rather than nourishes it.

Be determined to look good again and start doing something about it. After all, how can you expect your spouse to be attracted to you if you look unappealing?

2. Groom well.

Think about how you look on a daily basis. Get a nice haircut. Groom yourself as if you're preparing to meet the most important person in the world. Because you are - your spouse!

3. Dress well.

Pay attention to the clothes you put on each day. Not just for your work, but for your leisure time as well. It might be time to get rid of those 'old threads' that you just 'fall into' when you're around your house. Dress to impress - all the time.

* * *

Develop healthier habits. You'll not only feel better - and better about yourself - but your spouse will feel better about you as well. For so many people, the only time they put an effort into how they look is when they're going out socializing. It seems as if they're only willing to put in an effort to impress somebody other than their spouse.

But why would you want to impress a stranger more than you would the most important person in your life?

#2: Creating an Attractive Personality

Just as with a physical body - but perhaps even more so - when a marriage begins to be affected by the pressures and stresses of life, most people tend to put in less effort to creating and maintaining an attractive personality.

Ask yourself honestly:

*"Am I fun to be around? Am I the sort of person **I** would want to be around?"*

There are many ways to be fun to be around and to have a more attractive personality. Here are some of them:

1. Be a positive person.

There's so much negativity in the world today - why not be different?

It has been estimated that only 2% of people are positive and 98% are negative in their general attitude. Be a part of the 2%. Be positive and optimistic about your marriage and your life in general.

Develop the attitude:

"I'm not going to read the news and be depressed by all of the negativity.

I'm going to focus on the positive things in my life and in the world, because a lot of good positive things are there.

I'm going to be an optimist. I'm going to be the sort of person that people want to be around because I have a positive attitude that makes me - and them - feel good."

It's amazing what a positive attitude can do, not just for others but for yourself as well. You feel better, and the better you feel the better those around you will feel, including your spouse.

2. Be easy about life.

Don't be a 'drama king or queen' and make a big deal out of everything. Don't put so much pressure on yourself and other people.

Don't take life so seriously. Practice letting things go, without saying anything or trying to change what happens.

You'll begin to see that most things really aren't that important - and certainly not more important than you (and those around you) feeling good.

3. Be interesting.

When was the last time you and your spouse had a conversation about something interesting?

Make a habit of talking about interesting things rather than your problems (which, believe me, are *not* interesting). It might be a new idea you thought of yourself or which you got from someone else.

Also, understand that positive talk is interesting, negative talk is not. If you're the sort of person who only ever complains and talks about what's wrong with everything in their life and in the world, how likely is it that others are going to want to be around you?

It's very unlikely, unless those people are themselves not interesting or attractive either.

Become an interesting person - someone who makes conversation that is both interesting and positive - and other people (including your spouse) *are* going to be interested in seeking out and enjoying your company.

4. Be humorous and funny.

This is such an overlooked part of developing an attractive personality.

Become a joke teller. See the humorous side of life.

You don't need to overdo it and become tiresome or 'corny'. But enjoying the feeling of laughing - and making others laugh - is something you want to make a regular part of your life.

#3: Creating an Attractive Marriage

The third step in rebuilding passionate attraction (after you've focused on making yourself attractive both physically and in your personality) is to create an attractive relationship.

If your marriage is an attractive place to be - if it makes you and your spouse feel good - then it is going to create attraction between you. The passion will build naturally - just as it did in the early days of your relationship.

Here some effective ways to make your marriage more attractive:

1. Focus on the positive aspects of your marriage and your spouse.

I'm sure you did this early in your relationship. You overwhelmingly saw good things about your spouse.

So ask yourself:

"What are the good things about our marriage?"

"What's great about my spouse?"

That also means not focusing on your problems. If you focus on your problems, not only are you *not* going to feel good, but even if you do manage to solve the problems, you're just going to keep getting more of them.

Because:

Whatever you focus on, you get more of.

Where you choose to put your focus - and it **is** a choice - will determine **everything** you get in your life.

2. Accept your spouse for who they are.

Don't try and change your spouse. As we discussed in Chapter 2, it's virtually impossible to change someone else anyway.

Accept your spouse for who they are, instead of holding onto a picture of what they are not.

3. Lighten up your marriage.

Your marriage can be a fun and happy place. Work towards creating a marriage environment that relieves the pressures of your life, not adds to them.

If you feel tension rising between you and your spouse - stop.

Make a commitment to yourself and each other that you are going to stay away from drama in your marriage.

Creating negative drama is not worth it - and it's not necessary. So don't do it.

4. Show appreciation for your spouse.

As well as accepting your spouse for who they are, let them know that you appreciate them for who they are.

Tell your spouse that you appreciate them. **Do something** to show that you appreciate them.

If you are in a situation where your spouse is hostile towards you, you might be thinking:

"Why should I do that? After all, they don't show any appreciation towards me. And whenever I say or do something to show I appreciate them, I only get a negative reaction."

Your spouse may be hostile right now, but you have the power to change that by making the first move.

You don't need to show your appreciation in any way that is dramatic, forced, or complicated.

Just let them know that you're glad that you have them in your life.

Say or write to them something as simple as:

"I just want you to know that despite our problems, I'm glad to have you in my life."

5. Compliment don't criticize.

Eliminate your criticism from your marriage, no matter what you think, how justified your feel or how desperately you want to criticize. Just realize that if you criticize, it will only make the situation worse.

Instead of criticizing your spouse, develop the habit of paying them compliments instead. As long as you are genuine, you can praise and compliment them often.

Keep an eye out for things that they do (or have done) well. And let them know that you have noticed.

Say or write to them something like:

"I just want you to know that I really admire you for _____."

* * *

Make your marriage a safe place where you and your spouse can just be easy and relaxed with each other. After all, you both have enough problems everywhere else!

Create a marriage that is a 'haven', away from the world. A place where problems aren't the focus. A place where negativity doesn't exist. Make your marriage a place that you and your spouse escape **to**, rather than **from**.

Once you do, the attraction - and the passion - will return naturally.

* * *

As I said at the beginning of this chapter, passionate attraction isn't one of those mysterious or chemical things that you don't have any control over. If you were once attracted to your spouse and they were attracted to you, you can get that attraction back.

You simply need to focus on being an attractive person and doing attractive things. It all starts with you.

Don't let the words *"I'm simply not attracted to you anymore"* become a life sentence of unhappiness for you. With a little of the right effort, you can recapture the love, romance, passion and magic that you and your spouse once shared.

Chapter 6: How to Create Deep and Loving Communication
- by 'Doing the Opposite'

Deep and open communication is without doubt one of the most critical aspects of success in your marriage, which is why it is one of the Foundations of Uncounseling.

You might have already heard or read a lot about how to improve communication. There's a massive amount of information available, from books and videos to entire courses and seminars.

You may feel that when you encounter problems in your communication, the solution is to find new information - to learn and develop new and different techniques, methods, and skills.

However, great communication is not the result of techniques or methods. It doesn't come from developing new skills.

It is in fact simply the result of using communication in a 'certain way'.

Great marriages use this 'certain way' whereas other marriages do not.

In explaining this 'certain way', some of the ideas presented here might seem odd to you. Some may also appear to be rather basic or simplistic.

However, as you consider each idea, ask yourself the following two questions:

1. *"Does this describe what **was** happening when there was great communication in my marriage?"* (assuming that there was a time)

2. *"Is this something that **is no longer** happening in my marriage?"*

What is Communication - Really?

Before looking at how to create great communication in your marriage, let's understand clearly what communication actually is. The dictionary defines 'communication' as:

*"**The successful conveying or sharing of ideas and feelings.**"*

The key word in this definition is '**successful**.'

Success is measured by a **result**. Does your communication achieve the result you are looking for?

When you communicate with your spouse, do they respond to you in the way you want? Are their words and actions what you are wanting to hear and see?

This may seem obvious, but it is something that is often overlooked when thinking about communication.

When you are interacting with your spouse, your intention isn't for you to share an idea or feeling - only for them to ignore you or react negatively.

No, you are looking for **positive change** in them. You want them to respond to you by saying something or taking an action that will enhance and improve your relationship.

You want them to feel better about you, better about themselves, and you want your life to be better in some way.

Understanding this leads you to realize two important things:

1. Effective communication is not the result of what *you say*. It's the result of what *the other person hears*.

If the response that you get from your spouse is not what you want, then it's purely and simply because they are not hearing what you want them to hear. They are not interpreting your words in the way you intended.

2. The effectiveness of your communication with someone else is 100% *your* responsibility.

That means that if your spouse doesn't understand your message - if they don't respond in the way that you intended - then the fault lies with you.

It's not that they don't hear you right – it's that you are not saying it right.

And the solution to any misunderstanding can only come from you.

What You Need to Communicate in Your Marriage

In your attempts to communicate with your spouse, have you ever stopped to consider **what** it is that you're actually trying to get them to understand?

For your marriage to be happy and fulfilling, there are four things your spouse needs to know from you:

1. How you feel about yourself: what you want and need for you to be happy and fulfilled.

2. How you feel about them: that you love them for who they are and that you're attracted to them.

3. That you understand what they want and need to be happy and fulfilled.

4. That you respect their right to have what they want and need to be happy and fulfilled.

When you think about this, you will realize that these four things are at the heart of a successful marriage.

The Secret to Building *Great* Communication

If you wish to create great communication with your spouse, even if it has broken down completely, there are several things that you can do.

Each of these things is important, but there is one that is more important than anything else. It is, if you like, the 'magic ingredient' for great communication.

When I reveal what it is, your first reaction may well be that it seems to be so basic that perhaps there's a trick to it or that there's something more to it than there appears to be.

But there isn't. It is a simple concept, but despite that, it is one which very few people truly understand or are even aware of.

However, for this concept to make a difference in your life, it is not enough just to know what it is. You must apply it. This takes a bit more understanding and effort and it will be the subject of the rest of this chapter.

So here it is, the 'magic key' to creating great communication in your marriage:

You must get your spouse to *want* to communicate with you.

That's it.

99% of great communication comes from the *willingness* and *desire* of two people to understand each other.

If you really think about this, you'll realize that it is absolutely true - and here is a way to prove it to yourself.

Think back to the early days of your relationship. Wasn't it true that at that time you and your spouse *wanted* to communicate with each other?

You *wanted* to know what each was thinking, you were open to each other. You enjoyed learning about each other's thoughts, feelings, needs and desires.

You also respected their feelings, beliefs and opinions. You didn't get angry or frustrated or battle with them to change their mind or get them to see things 'your way'.

And if there was some misunderstanding or difference of opinion - if something wasn't clear - you each took the time to continue communicating until it was clear and you reached agreement.

Another feature of effective communication (based on willingness and desire) is a lack of antagonism, hostility or ill feeling.

There is no resistance. Communication continues - with love, enthusiasm, goodwill, respect and genuine interest - until the right message is conveyed.

It may require discussion, repetition, or rephrasing, but the goal of both parties is for true understanding - and they don't stop until that is achieved.

However, what happens when a marriage is not going well? People lose their *desire* and *willingness* to communicate openly and honestly. Instead, they replace it with resistance and resentment.

Often this is compounded by the fact that much of the so-called 'communication' that does exist tends to be about negative things, such as the problems in the marriage.

When a marriage is encountering difficulties, one spouse may be willing to communicate, but the other isn't. One person wants to maintain, and even increase, the level of communication but they meet with resistance from their spouse.

For the willingness and desire to communicate in your marriage to return, you need to recreate the 'atmosphere' as it was in your early days when things were going well. It is as simple as that.

And remember, creating great communication is **your** responsibility, not your spouse's. If you're willing to accept that, you can transform your communication - and your marriage.

The Link Between Attraction and Communication

There is a deep connection between creating attraction (as discussed in the previous chapter) and creating great communication. They are, in fact, two sides of the same coin.

This is because one of the keys to getting your spouse to want to communicate with you is to have them feel attracted to you. The more attractive you are, the greater your spouse's desire will be to communicate with you.

As a result of this, you will find an overlap in the ideas shared in this chapter with the chapter on attraction.

However, although similar, your strategies for rebuilding attraction and creating great communication will have different nuances.

They must be treated as separate 'projects' to achieve the best results for both. That is why, despite the overlaps, they are covered separately in two different chapters.

The Seven Elements of Great Communication in Your Marriage

Here are the seven things you need to work on to bring back the willingness and desire of your spouse to communicate with you.

By doing these things, you will get your spouse interested enough to see communicating with you as a pleasure rather than something to be endured or avoided.

Element #1: Feeling good about yourself

I've discussed this several times in this book, but the truth is, if you want your spouse to feel good about you, then you must feel good about yourself.

Why is it so important to feel good about yourself? In simple terms, when you feel good about yourself, you're happy.

When you're a happy person, you're a fun person, you're good to be around. Everyone - including your spouse - wants to be around fun and happy people.

No-one wants to be around a person who's miserable, who doesn't like their life, doesn't like themself, and doesn't do anything about improving their life and how they feel.

We all like to be around people who feel good about themselves, because it makes *us* feel good. So it stands to reason that it's going to make your spouse feel good when you're feeling good about yourself.

Of course, it isn't necessarily easy to feel good about yourself. In fact, remarkably few people really do. And acquiring a love for yourself can take a lifetime.

You will recall that the first Foundation of Uncounseling is to understand who you really are. The more you understand who you really are, the more that you will see the positive and unique qualities that are at your core. And the more you see these, the more you will like and appreciate yourself.

This is not vanity or arrogance. It's an understanding of yourself that is healthy, and which improves your life and the life of others.

You are, at your essence, a wonderful human being, worthy of love and all the best that life has to offer. You just need to see it.

Begin to see the good that is within you by answering the following questions:

- What's good about you?

- What are your positive qualities?

- What do others say that they admire about you, or what do you think they admire about you?

- What do you admire about yourself?

- What are some of the things that you've achieved or done in your life that you're proud of?

Create a written list of your answers and make it as long as you can. If you're truly honest with yourself, it will be a long list! You will see just how great you really are!

Element #2: Making your spouse feel good about themselves

Although you are not responsible for how your spouse feels, you can be a strong influence in making them feel good about themselves. When you do that - coming from a place where you feel good about yourself first - the effect can be very powerful.

Someone once said:

"Marriage is a mutual admiration society whose purpose is for two people to make each other feel good."

This is true. The whole point of being in a marriage is to feel good. What other reason is there to be there?

Problems and conflict only begin to appear when one or both spouses stops feeling good.

When you realize that your 'job' is simply to do your best to make your spouse feel good - while making sure you feel good about yourself - then that means you're going to have to act quite differently to the way you probably are right now.

Here are some of the ways that you can start to make your spouse feel good.

1. Accept everything your spouse says and does.

If you're in a place where you feel good about yourself, why not just accept everything they say and do? It doesn't matter what it is, or whether it is right or wrong.

Your marriage doesn't need to be a competition in seeing which one of you is right. In most cases, being right about something really doesn't matter and who knows what right or wrong is anyway?

Usually right and wrong is a matter of perspective, and nations have fought wars over whose perspective was right or wrong.

So, if your husband or wife says to you that they want to leave, say to them:

"If that is what you want to do, that's up to you. I cannot stop you."

If your spouse criticizes you and tells you what is 'wrong' with you and your marriage, just say,

"Thank you. I accept what you are saying."

Don't react negatively. Don't shout or try to prove to them that they are wrong. Don't try to justify yourself or your actions. Don't retaliate or do anything to 'get back' at them.

Now, of course you're probably thinking,

"But what if I really don't agree with my spouse? What if what they want isn't what I want?"

Of course, you are not necessarily going to **agree** with everything your spouse says or does, even if you say you accept it.

But by refusing to disagree with them you are simply acknowledging their right to say or do what they want.

If you really don't find their words or actions acceptable, your time will come to show them - but that time is not now.

To be able to demonstrate to your spouse - with sincerity and love - that you accept whatever they say and do, you need three things.

Firstly, you need to be working on feeling good about yourself, irrespective of what your spouse says or does (see Step #1 above).

Secondly, you need to examine **why** you can't accept what they are saying or doing.

Usually, the reason why you can't accept something that your spouse says or does is because of some fear that you have.

Are you afraid of being hurt in some way? Do you think that what they say or do is going to lead to something unpleasant happening? Do you think that you must get them to see that they are wrong?

In the final chapter of this book, you will learn a powerful process to remove your fears about what your spouse says and does and how it affects your life. That will help you be much more agreeable towards them.

Thirdly, you need to think about this: if you don't accept everything your spouse says or does, you're only going to create **hostility**.

Hostility only makes things worse. It never, ever makes things better. It only builds a bigger wall between you and your spouse and pushes them even further away.

What's the quickest way to stop hostility? Just accept and agree with them, or at least appear to.

In doing so you take away any possible reasons why they should feel hostile towards you.

What does it matter if you think their words or actions are wrong? You don't need to point that out.

You don't need to argue with your spouse. You don't need to try to convince them that they are wrong.

In the grand scheme of things, words and actions are insignificant. All that matters is how you (and they) feel.

Another very important benefit of agreeing with your spouse, is that you are showing them that you **respect** them.

You demonstrate that you accept that they are entitled to have a different viewpoint to you, and to carry out their own actions.

Of course, you must deal with the consequences of their actions or words as far as they affect you.

But disagreeing with your spouse is not going to achieve anything positive when it comes to improving the communication between you.

There is one caveat here. I'm not suggesting you *approve* of everything your spouse says or does.

I'm also not suggesting that you allow yourself to be manipulated by them or do things which are not in your best interests, or which may harm you.

But if you feel good about yourself - and have removed your fears - you can express your unwillingness to go along with them - whilst still accepting their right to their own opinions or actions. And you will see that for most things, agreeing with them is really not a big deal.

2. Don't criticize your spouse.

Criticism never changes anyone. So stop criticizing your spouse. Sometimes you might find this difficult. If you feel yourself wanting to criticize, change your focus.

Look or walk away.

Think about something else - something that makes you feel good. Recall something you are grateful for in your life.

Don't ignore *them*, of course, but if they say or do something you don't like, just let it go.

You will soon realize that the urge to criticize is simply a habit - and a habit which, when you break it, improves the quality of your marriage.

3. Praise your spouse for their good points.

Pay your spouse a **sincere** compliment.

After all, isn't that what you did early in your relationship?

You saw the good in them rather than their faults. You were liberal in your praise for what you admired about them and what they did well.

Shower them with your heartfelt praise again. Don't overdo it. Make sure it is genuine. But make sure you do it.

* * *

The more you can make your spouse feel good about themselves, the better they will feel about you - and the more they will be motivated to improve the communication - and your marriage.

But the more you criticize, are negative and make them feel bad and hostile, the more they're going to head in the opposite direction.

Element #3: Being interesting

We discussed this in the previous chapter on Attraction.

If you want your spouse to be interest**ed**, you must be interest**ing**. If you want to get their attention, your words and actions must be worthy of their attention.

Find interesting things to talk about. Find interesting things to do.

And share them with your spouse.

Element #4: Being positive in what you *think* and *say*

Confine your thoughts and words, as far as you are able, to things that are positive. You will be amazed at the effect this will have on your marriage and your life.

When people are having problems in their marriage, all they tend to think and talk about is their problems and how to fix them. This is a bad habit to get into and it won't help.

Remember again:

Whatever you focus on, you get more of.

Who enjoys listening to you criticizing, complaining or being negative? No-one - not even your spouse! And not yourself either!

I don't mean here that you should deny that things aren't going as well in your relationship as you would like. But if you really want to solve your problems, the way to do that is to focus on the solutions. It's doing the opposite!

Decide what you want, see a clear picture of what you want and ask yourself:

"*How can I get there?*"

This is a very different approach to saying:

"*I've got all these problems. I can't see how I'm going to solve them.*"

Focus on the good that you want, not the bad that you have. Look for the positive, not the negative. And express this positivity in your thoughts and words.

Element #5: Being positive in what you *do*

Your non-verbal communication is even more important than your verbal communication.

Think back to the early days of your relationship. What did you **do** then that was positive and fun that didn't involve words?

It probably included some playful touch or doing fun activities together sharing common interests.

Think of a couple of those things - and start doing them again.

One of the most basic ways to communicate nonverbally in a positive way is to smile! It is amazing the number of people in a marriage with poor communication who haven't smiled at their spouse in a long time.

Of course, it's not always easy to smile at your spouse when you're in a downward spiral of negativity in your relationship.

But do the opposite! Smile often and well. Be playful. And above all be genuine. It will make a big difference.

Element #6: Being fearless

To be fearless is to say and do what you think is right.

It will be the 'wrong' thing from time to time. Your spouse will misunderstand you. They will get upset sometimes. They will not like some of the things you say or do.

You will say or do something that you later regret. You will act out of anger or frustration sometimes.

Things won't always go the way you want or intend them to.

But don't be afraid of any of these things happening.

Don't let fear stop you from speaking or acting in a way that you think is right or which gives you pleasure.

Be honest and open - it's the best way to get your spouse to be honest and open with you.

Element #7: Being cheerful

Be someone who other people enjoy talking to and interacting with. Fill your life with compassion and warmth towards others.

Recognize that there is good in everyone and that everyone is doing their best - including both you and your spouse.

Of course, everyone has bad moments and days. You won't feel cheerful all the time. When that happens - fake it!

As the saying goes, *Fake it 'til you make it.'* There's a lot to be said for acting in a cheerful way when you don't feel it.

If you need a way to cheer yourself up and snap yourself out of a negative space, think back to the list you've created from Step #1 above: the list of all the good things about you, the things that you've achieved in your life and all the things you can be grateful for. It should be enough to cheer anyone up!

* * *

When you apply the Seven Elements in this chapter, you will become the sort of person your spouse wants to communicate with again. They will once again display a willingness and desire to listen to and understand what it is that you think and feel.

Your spouse will respond to you in a different, more constructive way and it's all because **you** are different: self-confident, supportive, positive in what you think, say and do, interesting, fearless and cheerful.

True communication doesn't take any skill or clever techniques. All it takes is a mutual desire for two people to understand each other.

That is why even people who speak entirely different languages can begin to communicate in a very short period of time, without knowing the meaning of the words that they are hearing. It's because they **want** to.

Most people try to force communication on their spouse.

Do the opposite: get your spouse wanting to communicate with you.

Create the right atmosphere and environment to allow true communication to happen in your marriage. And watch your marriage flourish as a result.

Chapter 7: An Unwilling Spouse? How to Win Them Over

What do you do when you want to heal your marriage, but your spouse is against it?

If you're in that situation, you'll know this is a very big problem. If your spouse has moved on - physically, emotionally or both - they might not only be unwilling to co-operate, but you trying to get them to commit to your marriage might make them angry and make matters even worse.

They may be telling you they want to leave, and no amount of trying seems to be able to get them to change their mind. Or you may simply be feeling that your marriage could be a lot better than it is, if only the two of you could 'work on it' together - yet your spouse is skeptical or not interested.

Traditional counseling can be helpful when both partners realize they have a problem and want to work together to heal the marriage.

But it's not an effective option when one person feels that it would be a waste of time, has given up, or is already on the way out the door and doesn't want to come back.

If you have a spouse who is stonewalling you, and even asking for a divorce, this chapter will help you to see things in a new way to regain the happy marriage that you want to have.

Healing A Marriage With an Unwilling Spouse

There are many reasons why your spouse might not want to be as committed as you are (or even hostile) to healing your marriage. Here are the most common. See which of these best describe your situation:

1. **Your spouse thinks that your marriage cannot be healed.**

   Perhaps you've tried counseling and it didn't work (it may have even made things worse). Your spouse might simply have given up on trying before you have.

2. **Your spouse is tired of all the unpleasantness in your marriage.**

   You are probably both feeling stressed and emotionally wrung out. So, they might be thinking that it would just be easier to call it quits and simply walk away, or stay, but in an unfulfilling marriage and leaving things the way they are.

3. **Your spouse is feeling bitter and hurt.**

   Perhaps you've done something that they feel has hurt them, and they just can't forgive you for it. You might have had an affair, been emotionally abusive or betrayed their trust in other ways. It seems that no matter what you do, you can't convince them that you are sorry for what has happened and that you will not act that way again.

4. **Your spouse no longer feels attracted to you.**

    They may be saying to you:
    "I love you, but I'm not in love with you".

5. **Your spouse has moved on emotionally.**

    They might have had (or be having) an affair or be romantically involved with somebody else. They could have even moved out or are making plans to move out.

Fortunately, there is a way to get your spouse to change their mind, and this has been a major theme of this book: you need to appeal to their emotions, not their logic.

You need to change their **feelings** about you and your marriage.

What *Not* To Do to Heal Your Marriage

Before we look at what you *should* do to win over your resistant spouse, let's look at what you should *not* do.

Not doing the *wrong* things is as important *as* doing the *right* things.

If you are doing any of the things listed here, you will be sabotaging your efforts to heal your marriage, perhaps without even realizing it.

Don't suggest counseling together

There are several reasons why suggesting counseling to your spouse might be a bad idea.

For a start, you might have already tried counseling and found that it didn't help. In fact, it could have even made things worse. So, if you're going to suggest you try it again, that suggestion is simply going to push your spouse further away from you.

They may think:

"We tried that, and it didn't work so what is the point of trying it again?

If that is all you can suggest for our marriage, then you're obviously not serious about healing it."

If the counseling you had was a futile or bad experience for your spouse, they are hardly going to be willing to give it another try.

Don't beg your spouse to stay or 'work on' your marriage

Don't plead, nag or beg them to stay with you or to 'work on' your marriage. Don't try to argue with them or give them logical reasons as to why they should.

Also:

Don't tell them they **need** to:

"We need to do this for the sake of the children/for the sake of the past/for the sake of the future."

Don't appear dependent on them:

"I can't live without you. If we don't heal our marriage, I wouldn't know what to do. I wouldn't be able to cope."

If you are using any of these 'scripts' (or anything like them), stop. They will only make things worse.

Don't try to make your spouse feel guilty about not 'working on' your marriage

Don't tell your spouse that they are wrong, that they are selfish, mean, they don't care about the family or you, and so on.

If you try to use guilt as a tactic you will probably only end up making them feel resentful.

Don't say:

- *"You are so selfish. You don't care about anyone other than yourself."*
- *"Everyone in your family thinks you should stay/work on our marriage."*
- *"You are letting everyone down by your attitude."*

Using guilt is a very destructive tool that always backfires.

Don't threaten your spouse

Many people, in their desperation, threaten their spouse with dire consequences if they leave or don't work on the marriage.

These could be financial threats: *"If you leave, I'll make sure that you won't get your share of the money,"* or *"I'll make it hard for you financially."*

Another type of threat involves the children: *"If you leave, I'll make sure you don't get to see the children, or not as often as you would like."*

It could be a threat to their reputation: *"If you leave or don't work on our marriage with me, I'll tell everyone how bad you are. I'll tell your work colleagues, your professional circle, your friends, your family. Basically, I'm going to tell everyone that you are a bad person because you left me."*

You may threaten to end the marriage yourself. *"If you don't work on this with me, I'm going to leave."*

Some people even threaten their spouse with harming themselves: *"If you do this to me or if we can't heal our marriage, I'm going to kill myself,"* or *"I'm going to hurt myself."*

These are just some of the different types of threats that many people use. They are all entirely counterproductive and will not help your situation one iota.

Don't become distant or cold towards your spouse

This can be very difficult because you're probably feeling hurt, betrayed and bitter. However, in effect, what you're doing when you are distant or cold is that you are using another way to try to punish your spouse for their unwillingness to do what you want.

When you work on the more positive aspects of what to **do** rather than what **not** to do (which we will look at next), you will find that your tendency to be distant and cold will diminish.

However, realize that being distant or cold only makes your spouse dislike or resent you even more.

* * *

Why is it that you shouldn't do any of these things? Why they are all counterproductive to healing your marriage?

The main reason is obvious. By adopting any of these behaviors, all you are doing is creating more negative *feelings*.

Remember, negative feelings are the reason why your spouse wants to leave or resist you in the first place. By making them feel worse you are only going to push them away further and faster.

The other reason you don't want to do these things is they make you appear weak and desperate. When you appear weak, you become very unattractive. And you don't want to be less attractive to your spouse. You want to be *more* attractive.

This is a vital point to understand: if you want your spouse to commit to your marriage, then you must give them an incentive to do so.

A marriage with you should appear to them as their best option for being happy. This is particularly true if there is another person involved (in other words if your spouse is having an affair). If you are competing with someone else, then your goal is to be more attractive to your spouse than they are.

So, the key to changing your spouse from unwilling to willing is to create positive feelings and emotions around your marriage, not negative ones.

And the first step is to stop doing the things that are creating the negativity.

What *To* Do to Heal Your Marriage

Once you've stopped doing all the **wrong** things, it's time to replace them with the **right** things.

As with many of the ideas in this book, what I'm about to share with you might seem straightforward, or even obvious. But while these ideas are simple, that doesn't mean they are necessarily easy to implement. That will require some effort and discipline on your part.

Step #1: Make the Decision that you will heal your marriage

If you have decided (from Chapter 3) that your marriage is - and continues to be - right for you, then you must commit to healing it.

However, there is a big difference between *wanting* to or *hoping* to heal your marriage - and ***committing*** to the outcome.

Hope and want are both very weak. But commitment - which means doing whatever it takes and not giving up until you achieve your goal - is powerful.

And that power and strength is what will carry you through to the right result.

So ask yourself:

"Do I hope and want to heal my marriage? Or am I committed to it?"

Step #2: Work on yourself

You will recall from the first Foundation of Uncounseling in Chapter 2 that:

You can never fix anything in your life (including your marriage) by trying to fix it.

You can only fix something by fixing *yourself*.

Trying to fix your marriage doesn't work. Fixing yourself does.

So all of your work and attention should be on improving yourself.

Become a person worthy of a great marriage - and that is what you will get.

Here are some of the ways to work on yourself:

1. Put your own happiness first.

From the exercises from Chapter 3, you should be getting clear about what it is that makes you happy. Whatever it is, start doing the things that will create happiness in your life.

It is essential to put your own happiness first. This might seem a foreign concept. Unfortunately, through our cultural conditioning and what we've been taught, we often have the idea that marriage is all about sacrifice and putting our own needs last. The opposite is true. When you put yourself first you are not being 'selfish'. You are living your life purpose, which is to be happy.

You cannot make anyone else happy unless you yourself are happy. The happier you are the more you will give happiness to others. The more you will be productive, creative, generous, loving and compassionate – all of which improves the lives of others as well as your own.

So whatever it is that you love to do, if it doesn't harm others, start doing it.

2. Develop your social life.

When times get tough, people often retreat inside themselves and reduce their time with other people. You should do the opposite. Get out and have some fun, even if you don't feel like it. If there are friends whose company you enjoy, socialize more often with them.

If you don't have much of a social network, define the sorts of people you would like to have as friends and go out and find them.

Many people feel guilty about doing this. They feel that enjoying themselves is not 'appropriate'. They are concerned that it might be sending the message that they are not taking their marriage problems seriously.

But remember, the best thing you can do for your marriage is to be happy!

Having fun with other people is one of the best ways to do that.

3. Work on developing the Ideal You.

- How do you want to be perceived by other people?

- How would you like others to describe you?

- Imagine yourself at your own funeral. What would you like to hear being said about you and your life?

Do you want to be seen as someone who is strong? Loving? Forgiving? Gentle? Faithful? Determined? Happy? Easygoing? Positive? What are the qualities that you would like other people to notice about you and for them to say, *"What a great person they are!"*

Once you have defined the qualities of the Ideal You, start creating them in your life. There are many ways you can do this. One is to take all of the questions and exercises in this book very seriously. They are all about helping you turn yourself into the best version of You.

As you work on creating the Ideal You, be very aware of your thoughts and behaviors. Is the way you are thinking, speaking and acting in line with the Ideal You?

For instance, if you want to be determined, happy and loving start to think and act in that way.

Step #3: Work *towards* a happy marriage, not *away* from an unhappy one

Whatever you focus on you get more of.

If you focus on your problems, you will get more problems.

If you focus on what is good about your life and your marriage, you will get more that is good.

Counseling: Negative focus - solving problems.

Uncounseling: Positive focus - expanding the good.

A positive focus is much more than positive thinking. In fact, positive thinking in itself generally doesn't work.

This is because when you are trying to 'think positive' what you are usually doing in reality is thinking and feeling 'negative'.

You are trying to cover over those negative thoughts and feelings with positive words and statements. You're trying to trick yourself into believing them. But it's not what you're really thinking - and it's certainly not what you're feeling.

Trying to fake it is not positive thinking.

So, forget about trying to 'think positive' and instead do the things that will create more positive outcomes in your life. Then your thinking will automatically become more positive.

Two of the most powerful things you can do to change your focus from negative to positive are:

1. Do not react to negativity.

If your spouse says or does something negative, try not to react to it. Be aware that if you do, you are only adding more negative energy to the situation.

Make a point of refusing to participate in an argument.

Do whatever it takes.

Change the subject. Become silent. Walk away.

If you feel yourself being drawn into an argument, don't try and be the one who wins, because the only outcome will be that neither of you will win. Both of you will feel bad.

It is not weak to walk away from an argument or to simply refuse to get into one. In fact, it is a sign of true strength.

Knowing when to walk away is Wisdom.
Being able to walk away is Courage.
Walking away with your head held high is
Dignity.

-Bohdi Sanders

If you can train yourself to stop reacting to negativity you will see a major improvement in your marriage (and your life) situation.

2. Forgive unconditionally.

How willing are you to forgive your spouse for *all* the things they have done to hurt you?

The word 'unconditional' means without *any* strings attached - at all.

Your spouse doesn't have to do something (or not do something), or behave in a certain way, for you to forgive them.

Your forgiveness is not dependent on anything that they say or do.

They don't have to change for you to forgive them.

This also means you have no negative expectations for the future.

You are not concerned that if you forgive your spouse now, they may do something later that will hurt you again.

This may sound difficult to do. But true and unconditional forgiveness is what will heal you and your marriage.

Step #4: Don't be dependent on your marriage for your happiness

Marriage dependency is a trap which many people fall into. They say:

"I can't be happy unless I am married to this person."

"I can't be happy until we solve our marriage problems."

This is a destructive attitude. When you make your marriage responsible for your happiness you play a futile game. Your marriage can never make you happy - only **you** can make you happy.

When you give over responsibility for your happiness to your marriage and your spouse, you also appear weak.

This makes you less attractive to your spouse. Your spouse will not respect or admire you if you lack confidence or belief in yourself - and are instead blaming them or your marriage for how you feel.

You must find a way to know, in your mind, that you **can** and **will** be happy in your life, irrespective of what's going on in your marriage right now or what may happen in the future.

This also means that you must be willing to let go of your marriage if you know that it's never going to make you happy (refer back to Chapter 3).

Ironically, if your spouse knows that you are willing to let go of your marriage, it often will have a very positive effect on them.

If they stop feeling any pressure from you, they will feel better, both about you and themselves. That can cause them to look more favorably on your marriage - and they may even decide to work through the healing process with you.

Think back to the picture of your Ideal Marriage that you created in the exercise in Chapter 4. See yourself once again leading a happy life - *without* your marriage.

When you build a picture in your mind of a happy life without your marriage, you are showing yourself that it's possible.

This will help you remove the feelings of dependency on your marriage for you to be happy - and your marriage will improve as a result.

Step #5: Be attractive

It is vital to realize that the results you get in your life depend on the energy you put out.

The more positive energy you radiate, the more attractive you will be.

In Chapter 5, and in fact throughout this book, we have explored many ways to make yourself more attractive to your spouse.

The more attractive you are, the faster you will heal your marriage - irrespective of how your marriage is right now.

Step #6: Create opportunities to connect positively with your spouse

If you're continually putting negative energy into your marriage, you're only going to keep getting more of it.

You need to break the cycle of negativity and re-establish a positive connection with your spouse.

Here are a couple of quick and effective ways to do this.

1. Make your spouse laugh. This is so basic, but so few people do this, especially when they are having problems.

   Find something to laugh about. It doesn't matter if it's silly - at the very least it may result in some rolling eyeballs, which is halfway to a laugh.

2. Recall and share a positive moment from your past together.

   What were some of the great times you've had as a couple?

   Think of something humorous, positive or exciting that you did in the past and share the memory.

   Put a smile on your face and say to your spouse:

   "Do you remember the time when...... It was fun wasn't it?"

Laughing and recalling some good times are two great ways to connect with your spouse is a positive way.

Step #7: Don't give up

This is perhaps the most important step of all and it relates right back to your commitment to healing your marriage in Step #1.

Healing your marriage may not be easy.

It will be all the more difficult when it appears that your spouse is working against you rather than with you.

You will experience setbacks. You may endure more heartbreak, pain and disappointment. You may find yourself losing the motivation to carry on at times.

However, most people give up on something just before they would have succeeded. This is true of everything in life, not just healing a relationship.

There is light at the end of the tunnel. But there is often a bend in the tunnel just before the end, so that you can't see the light until you're almost there. You're closer to your success than you realize.

Of course, at some point you may decide that your situation is hopeless. There may come a time when you no longer feel deep in your heart that your marriage is right for you.

If that is the case, you simply must overcome your fears about moving on and do so.

There is no shame in changing your mind about your marriage when the circumstances are no longer right for you. Be willing to stay true to yourself by moving in a different direction if and when necessary.

Doing what you think is best at all times is a sign of courage and strength, not weakness.

But if you continue to know that healing your marriage is right for you and your spouse, do the things I suggest in this book. If something doesn't work the first time, do it again.

Modify your approach if you think you need to. Get more help and support if you think you need it. And above all, continue to use the Uncounseling approach to work on yourself.

As long as it continues to feel right for you to heal your marriage, promise yourself you will never give up until you succeed.

The Marriage Success Mindset

Adopt the following seven thoughts as your own mindset. They will help you to maintain the positive energy which is essential for your success.

1. *"I am going to heal our marriage. It feels right. I love my spouse and I'll do whatever it takes to do this."*

2. *"I am a great person, worthy of love and of having a happy and fulfilling life."*

3. *"I create my own happiness."*

4. *"I am not dependent on my marriage for me to be happy."*

5. *"I am attractive - physically, mentally, emotionally and sexually. I work on becoming more attractive every day."*

6. *"I focus on the positive aspects of our marriage."*

7. *"Our marriage can and will get better."*

The Four Keys to Marriage Success

1. Maintain positive energy.

The energy you put out is what you will get back.

2. Love your spouse unconditionally.

Look beyond your spouse's words and actions. Whatever they say or do, remember that they are just doing their best to meet their own needs, as indeed you are. Love and respect them for that.

3. Focus on your own self-worth.

Your own happiness is the most important thing. You are a worthy and worthwhile person.

4. Keep your goal in mind.

Stay focused on healing your marriage (while continuing to evaluate whether it is the right goal for you).

Chapter 8: Your 'Greatest Gifts' For Healing Your Marriage
- That Are Hidden in Plain Sight

There is something that you have in your life - that you have had all your life - that are your greatest gifts for healing your marriage.

But they are gifts that you have not only *not* recognized or appreciated, but you've actually tried to push them away.

And those gifts are:

Your mistakes.

Most people think that mistakes are somehow bad, and they will do everything they can to avoid making them.

This is in large part due to the conditioning received through our education system, where students are penalized for making mistakes and rewarded for a lack of mistakes (the fewer mistakes you make, the higher your grades).

This negative attitude (and even fear) towards mistakes carries through into adult life. It means that most people have the view that in their marriage, a mistake - everything from saying something hurtful to having an affair - is something that is harmful.

This is unfortunate, because it reflects a faulty perspective on what mistakes actually are.

If mistakes from the past or present are harming your marriage and creating hurt, guilt and unhappiness, realize it doesn't need to be that way.

Your mistakes can actually help your marriage. They can bring love and healing to your marriage instead of pain and destruction.

Yes, your mistakes can make your marriage better!

* * *

The truth is - and this is something we often forget in our marriage when something goes 'wrong' - *everyone* **makes mistakes.**

You may think that people in wonderful marriages somehow never (or hardly ever) make mistakes, or that they don't have the same problems as others. Or perhaps, they are 'different' or 'better' than other people.

But people who are in fulfilling marriages still may make a lot of mistakes. In fact, they often make more mistakes than the 'average' couple, because they are willing to take risks in their relationship.

However, how they **deal** with their mistakes is very different.

This difference essentially comes down to how they see their mistakes or, to put it another way, the **meaning** they attach to the word 'mistake.'

In fact, **what you think a mistake is (the meaning you give to it) will determine not only the quality of your marriage, but the quality of your life.**

In this chapter we are going to look at some of the different meanings given to the word 'mistake' and how they affect a marriage.

We'll also look at some of the things that you can do to change the role of 'mistakes' in your own marriage. By doing so, you will be able to deal with your mistakes in a way that improves rather than harms your relationship with your spouse.

As you will soon see, redefining 'mistakes' changes everything. And it works for all types of mistakes, irrespective of how trivial or major they might appear to be.

The 'mistake' could be something as potentially devastating as your spouse (or you) having an affair. Most people would consider that there is probably no bigger mistake a person can make in their marriage than to have an affair.

But it could also be something small and seemingly trivial that falls into the definition of 'mistake' that has had a negative impact on your marriage.

It could be losing your temper with your spouse, getting angry, shouting at them, saying something unpleasant, not considering their feelings, or being cold, hostile and non-communicative.

However, it is not the relative 'size' of the mistake that is important, it is the impact. In some marriages, 'small' mistakes can be the trigger for a divorce, perhaps even after the couple has lived through and survived a 'big' mistake, such as an affair.

The Negative Effects of Using Mistakes in the Wrong Way

As I have said, most people make the 'mistake' of seeing mistakes in the wrong way. This harms their marriage and their life.

The truth is that if any mistakes from the past in your marriage are causing you anything other than short-term pain, then you have been looking at them from the wrong perspective.

Here are the most common negative effects on your marriage from the wrong interpretation and use of the word 'mistake'.

Negative Effect #1: It keeps your marriage stuck in a negative space

Whatever you focus on, you get more of.

If you focus on a mistake - trying to get over it or trying to heal from it - what will you get more of?

More 'trying to get over it' and more 'trying to heal'. And more 'mistakes'.

Sometimes it does take some time and effort to forgive or to get over a mistake. But that can be reduced considerably by handling the mistake in a different way (which is what this chapter is about).

The important thing is that you don't want to keep your marriage stuck in negativity, which is what happens when you deal with mistakes in the wrong way.

Negative Effect #2: It weakens the person who made the mistake

Weakness is not something that is good for anyone, especially within the context of marriage. Being weak makes you unattractive, both to yourself and your spouse.

I'm sure you know this feeling:

You've made a mistake and you're trying to get your spouse to forgive you for it, or you yourself are feeling bad about it - and it makes you feel weak and bad about yourself. This is not going to be attractive to your spouse, and therefore it will be detrimental to your marriage.

Negative Effect #3: It creates an imbalance of power in the relationship

In every 'mistake' there are two people (at least) involved. One is the person who made the mistake (the perpetrator). The other is the so-called 'victim' of the mistake.

Handling mistakes in the wrong way creates an imbalance of power between perpetrator and victim. The person who made the mistake is made to feel bad, inferior and guilty. The expectation is that they must somehow earn the forgiveness of the victim.

This can lead to feelings of frustration, resentment and low self-esteem in the perpetrator. And it can create feelings of superiority, entitlement, disrespect and lack of self-responsibility in the victim.

None of these feelings are healthy for either person or for the marriage itself.

Negative Effect #4: It takes the couple away from where they want and need to be

Obviously, a mistake is something that happened in the past. But if you keep focusing on the mistake, it keeps your focus on the past as well. And that keeps you away from the only place that is important - the only place that even exists - which is the present moment. Being right here, right now.

A great marriage is built on a love of this moment and an optimism for the future. Looking at past mistakes in a way that causes you to feel unhappy will never help your present or your future.

What ARE Mistakes - Really?

Most of us have completely the wrong idea about what mistakes are, and this results in a huge amount of unnecessary pain.

To understand the true meaning and purpose of mistakes, let us start with a dictionary definition.

The dictionary defines the word 'mistake' as:

"An error or fault resulting from defective judgment, deficient knowledge, or carelessness."

The first part of this definition to note is 'defective judgement'. 'Defective' means something that is not perfect.

You know that already. But here's something that many people seem to have forgotten about:

No one has perfect judgement all of the time.

For us as human beings, perfect judgement is impossible. We simply can't see things as they really are all of the time. This cannot be avoided.

Next, there is 'deficient knowledge'. This means that mistakes come about because of things we don't know.

But here's the thing:

No-one has perfect knowledge.

No-one knows everything. And without knowing everything - without perfect knowledge - it is certain that you are not going to do the 'perfect thing' in every moment in your life.

Then there is the word 'carelessness'.

No one is careful all the time.

No-one can be thinking or paying full attention to everything 100% of the time. It's not realistic or even desirable.

Most 'mistakes' are the result, not of intentional action, but of carelessness.

Remember, it is your emotions, not your logical thoughts, that cause you to do what you do. This means that you will do things on impulse - being careless - rather than after thinking of the consequences. This is a natural part of being human.

These are three elements in the dictionary definition of the word 'mistake'.

However, this definition also contains clues as to what a mistake is **not**. These aren't stated overtly in the definition, but they are implied.

Firstly, **a mistake is usually not intentional.**

Very few people do something to intentionally hurt themself or someone else who they care about (such as their spouse).

Often we don't see the negative consequences of our actions. If we did - if we knew in advance the true extent of how our actions would hurt others or even ourselves - it is unlikely we would take that action (make that 'mistake').

Secondly, **a mistake is not permanent.**

A mistake is usually a one-off thing. It could be either a single incident or it could have been a situation that took place over a period (this might include a negative attitude you may hold towards your spouse or even having an affair).

It may repeat itself more than once, but each time it is a finite event. The mistake has a beginning - and an end.

Where the damage really occurs is when you hold onto the memory of the mistake, long after the actual mistake has ended.

If you continue to think about what happened, those thoughts will continue to make you feel upset or unhappy.

But the mistake is no longer actually there. The effects of the mistake will still be there - but only because you have chosen to keep those effects alive in your thoughts.

* * *

The dictionary definition is a useful starting point for understanding what mistakes really are. This understanding alone can lessen the impact of mistakes in your marriage.

But if you are finding that a mistake that you or your spouse has made in the past is having a negative effect on your marriage today - if the memory of it is still causing hurt and pain - then you need to know how you can change that.

The mistake happened. You can't change that.

But you can change the impact it continues to have on your relationship.

A New Definition for 'Mistake'

While the dictionary definition of the word 'mistake' is useful, it has its limitations. When you look at it closely, it portrays mistakes as only being negative in nature. A mistake looks like something to be avoided.

But in fact, people with great marriages - and indeed people with great lives - have a completely different definition of the word 'mistake.' Here it is:

Mistake: A Learning Experience that improves the quality of your life.

If you look at your mistakes in this way, you can see that they provide a huge opportunity to make your life (including your marriage) better.

Through your mistakes, you can become a better person, a better spouse, and create a better marriage.

After all, it's through your mistakes that you learn and improve anything.

You don't learn to ride a bicycle by reading a book about it, talking about it, or feeling excited or motivated.

You learn by doing - and by doing it wrong. You simply get on the bike. You fall off almost immediately (a 'mistake') but you keep trying. Each time you fall off you learn more about how to ride the bike - and you keep trying (making 'mistakes') until you master the skill and get the result you want — which is being able to ride a bicycle.

Learning is experiential, not theoretical. Success in anything comes from doing, doing it wrong, evaluating the results and continuing until you get it right.

Using Your Mistakes to Heal and Transform Your Marriage

Here is a list of things that you can do, that can transform your mistakes from something that harms your marriage into something that heals and improves it.

I call these Mistake Transformers. They will help you to experience 'mistakes' in a different way, and to use them to your benefit rather than your detriment.

Mistake Transformer #1: Acknowledge that you have made a mistake

When you make a mistake, acknowledge what you have done, both to your spouse and to yourself. It's as simple as saying, *"I made a mistake."*

By acknowledging, I don't mean justifying yourself. This isn't about coming up with reasons or a detailed analysis of **why** you acted the way you did or what it meant.

Simply say to yourself and to your spouse:

"I made a mistake - nothing more, nothing less." It's extremely important to make acknowledgement your first step because without it you remain stuck.

Mistake Transformer #2: Stop apologizing for the mistake

If you make a mistake, obviously you should apologize for it. But once is enough.

Continuing to remind your spouse (and yourself) that you're sorry for what happened is not going to make any positive difference to your situation.

All it will do is distract you from doing and thinking the things that **will** improve your marriage.

So, stop apologizing for your mistakes. And if your spouse continues to apologize for something they did, tell them to stop. Tell them it is not necessary; that you accept their apology and that they don't need to apologize again.

Mistake Transformer #3: Don't take responsibility for your spouse's feelings

It's important in a marriage relationship to do your best to make your spouse feel good. But this is very different to taking *responsibility* for how they feel.

If you or your spouse take responsibility for the other's feelings, there can never be true harmony in your relationship.

In fact, learning to take full and total responsibility for your **own** feelings is one of the greatest lessons you need to learn to achieve happiness and fulfillment in your life, as well as in your marriage.

As you take responsibility for your own feelings - also give your spouse the opportunity to be responsible for their feelings.

This may be difficult, at least to begin with. You may want to continue to blame your spouse for how you feel.

Your spouse may continue to blame you. They might keep wanting to make you feel guilty. They might continue to fuel negative emotion by reminding you of your 'mistake'.

Often a person refuses to take responsibility for their own feelings by continuing to dwell on a past mistake made by their spouse.

They may say things such as:

"I don't know if I can forgive you for what you did. I don't know if we can carry on. Because of what you did, it might mean the end of our marriage."

You or your spouse may also attach conditions to forgiveness:

"I can't forgive you until you (or unless you) _____"

The bottom line is this: how someone feels about anything is completely up to them. It's not anyone else's responsibility - or problem. It is all theirs.

Allow your spouse to learn how to be responsible for their own feelings while you learn how to be responsible for your own feelings.

If that is all that you did, your relationship would see a significant improvement.

How do you stop taking responsibility for your spouse's feelings? By simply refusing to allow them to make you feel bad through blame, resentment or anger.

If you are put in a situation where this may arise, simply say to them:

"I'm not responsible for how you feel. And I don't expect you to be responsible for how I feel."

And leave it at that.

Mistake Transformer #4: Look for the positive side of the mistake

Everything in this universe has two sides. There is up/down, in/out, hot/cold, positive/negative, light/dark, strong/weak – and many other examples.

There is also a positive side to a mistake. To find it, all you need to do is look for it.

Think of something in your marriage that you would call a mistake, something that has been causing you pain and distress. Ask yourself:

"If I really wanted to, what could I see that was good about that 'mistake'?"

"What have I learned from this experience? What has it taught me?"

"How could I use what I've learned to improve our relationship?"

"What good things could now happen in our marriage because of that 'mistake' having occurred?"

Very often mistakes are reminders of what's not right in your marriage. They are 'red flags', giving 'advance warning' of something that, if continued, could have disastrous effects on the marriage.

For instance, imagine if you were to become angry with your spouse and shout at them or say something unkind.

You might realize afterwards that it was a mistake to have behaved in that way. But the fact that you did lash out at them gives you an opportunity to identify **why** you did.

Perhaps it was because you were feeling stressed by something else going on in your life. Maybe you were resentful that your needs are not being met in your marriage.

Whatever it was, your mistake (lashing out at your spouse) had an underlying cause. Finding the cause, by digging deeper, would help you to see what needed to be addressed and corrected before it developed into bigger problems in your marriage.

So, using the above example, you would seek to reduce or eliminate the stresses from your life. Or you would work to having your needs met in your marriage, using the ideas in this book.

An affair is an interesting 'mistake' in this regard. If you or your spouse has had (or is having) an affair with somebody else, what does it mean? What's the positive side of an affair?

"How can there be a positive side to an affair?", I hear you say.

Remember, there are two sides to everything. Just because you can't see it doesn't mean it isn't there.

The fact is, an affair does have a positive side: it shows you what is missing in your marriage. It could be things such as fun, intimacy, excitement, doing things together and appreciating one another.

The 'mistake' of an affair can be a very powerful wakeup call for your marriage. It can be the catalyst for you to put your awareness and effort into those things which will make your marriage great, rather than just allowing your marriage to slide into complacency, misery and even divorce.

Ask yourself the questions above to see the positive side to your mistakes. You will be amazed at what you'll discover - and how helpful it will be for you and your marriage.

Mistake Transformer #5: Expect *more* mistakes

Once you see mistakes as learning opportunities and gifts, you can almost look forward to more of them!

This is something that you see in people who've achieved a great deal in their life and who are happy.

They are grateful for every opportunity to learn from their mistakes and they aren't afraid of making more. They realize that what they learn from their mistakes helps them improve their life.

As a human being, you know that you're going to make more mistakes in your life. That is inevitable.

But you have a choice as to how you view those mistakes and what you do as a result.

Do you choose to see your mistakes (and the mistakes of others, including your spouse) as negative and harmful - in which case you spend your time being afraid of them and trying to avoid them?

Or do you see mistakes for what they really are: the gift of an opportunity to learn something to create a happier marriage and a better life?

When Thomas Edison was trying to invent the light bulb, he tried thousands of different materials before he was able to make one work. Before he finally succeeded, his assistant said to him:

"All our hard work is in vain. We have gained nothing."

His reply was very telling:

"We have come a long way and we have learned a lot. We know that there are 2,000 elements that cannot make a good light bulb."

Wouldn't that be a wonderful attitude to have about mistakes in your marriage? Nothing you do can ever be wrong. It can only be a learning opportunity, something which takes you one step closer to creating the wonderful relationship that you really want to have.

What this really boils down to is this:

Happiness and success in your marriage and your life is not the result of *what* happens. Happiness and success is the result of the *meaning that you give* to what happens.

Because:

Nothing means anything other than the meaning you choose to give it.

Whatever you choose to think something **means** - and it is a choice - will determine whether it is positive or negative. You, and you alone, decide which.

That meaning will determine how you feel - either happy or unhappy.

In turn, how you feel will determine what you do. If you feel good, you will take positive, constructive actions that will help improve your life. If you feel bad, you will take negative, destructive actions that will only create more unwanted results.

You may be thinking that your spouse might not share your 'new definition' of mistakes and that your marriage can't change without your spouse doing that. The truth is that your marriage can change without them changing, and it will.

Because all change in your life and your marriage must start with you. If your spouse is not responsive (or even hostile), once you begin to change yourself, they can't help but change as well.

* * *

The freedom to make mistakes is one of the most important elements of building true trust and intimacy in your marriage.

Don't let past mistakes destroy your marriage when they can be used to transform it. All it takes is a change in the meaning you give to the word 'mistake'. And it is a change that you have the power within you to make.

Chapter 9: The Ultimate Secret to Success in Your Marriage

Your task is not to seek for love, but merely
to seek and find all the barriers within
yourself that you have built against it.

- Rumi (13th Century Poet)

You may do all the things suggested in this book. You may be working on yourself first and your marriage second (which is the right order). And you may be seeing some incremental changes.

But despite all of this, perhaps you're not seeing the results you would really like. Or the progress you are making is not as fast as you had hoped.

If that is the case, then there is only one reason why you are not achieving the level of success that you want:

You are not _allowing_ success to happen.

You're trying too hard. You're trying to force results.

Force never works. Force is not a part of the natural flow of life. And it won't get you to where you want to go in your life either.

There is a big difference between **force** and *power*. True power never comes from struggle, pressure and trying to force an outcome, whether that be healing your marriage or getting anything else in your life.

True power comes from letting go and allowing the right results to come to you. And when you understand what letting go really is - and apply it - the right results *will* come to you.

Much more easily - and in ways you would never have imagined.

There is an 'unseen power' that comes with letting go and allowing. This power has been described by artists, philosophers, spiritual teachers and great achievers throughout history. It has been described as a feeling of 'being in the flow' or 'in the zone'. But whatever 'it' is, this same power has the ability to transform your marriage.

In this chapter you'll discover the true meaning of letting go. You'll see why it is the secret to success, what happens when you truly let go, what's stopping you from letting go and allowing your marriage to be healed and, most importantly, how to use the power that comes from letting go to get the results you want.

When you understand and apply the 'secret' of letting go, the results you achieve in your marriage (and life) will astound and delight you.

The Truth About Letting Go

Most people struggle with the idea of letting go because they have the wrong concept of what it is. They think that it means to give up control and put themselves at the mercy of other people, events and circumstances.

But true letting go is nothing like this. When you let go, you stay in control - but you transfer your control to the 'part of you' that knows what you want and can give it to you.

You allow that part of you to take over. This takes trust, which only comes from understanding what this part of you is and how it works.

Do you trust that the sun will rise tomorrow morning? Do you trust that you will continue to breathe and that your heart will continue to beat?

Of course you do. You don't worry that these things won't happen. But why do you trust? It's because you understand that these things are natural, and that they happen according to natural processes.

It's the same with your marriage. Once you understand how things work - that there is a part of you, an invisible power, whose job is to bring you what you truly want - you are able to let go and allow that power to heal your marriage (or give you whatever else is best for you).

If you don't fully understand this, don't worry. It will all become clear to you in this chapter.

What is Letting Go?

What does 'letting go' really mean in practical terms?

Put simply:

Letting Go is giving up attachment to a specific outcome.

In other words, you are open to all possibilities, knowing that the right things will show up in your life, and at the right time.

Most people who want to heal their marriage see 'fixing their marriage' as the only option they have for being happy.

But when you only have a single outcome that is acceptable to you, all that does is create stress and pressure upon yourself.

And what do stress, pressure, and other forms of negativity do? Of course, they make you and your marriage less attractive and desirable for your spouse.

When you let go, you take the pressure off yourself and your marriage.

You understand and accept that there are other options available to you. You know that your happiness can be achieved in ways other than staying married and healing your relationship.

This doesn't mean that you shouldn't **want** to heal your marriage. It doesn't mean you should stop putting in the effort to heal it. It also doesn't mean that your marriage is wrong for you.

But if you see fixing your marriage as the only positive outcome for you - the only way that you can see yourself being truly happy - then you will inevitably put all sorts of pressure on yourself.

This will create stress and struggle - and have you doing all the wrong things - things that take you away from your goal rather than towards it.

You know what those 'wrong things' are. Many of them have been described in this book.

When you only have one goal that is acceptable to you, you also limit yourself from seeing other opportunities, other options, and other ways of looking at and improving your life that ultimately could help you in your marriage as well.

There are many other possible positive outcomes available to you, other than healing your marriage.

They could include:

- Living a fulfilling and happy life alone.
- Having a loving relationship with someone else.
- Having an 'alternative marriage arrangement' with your spouse (e.g., remaining married to your spouse, but being in a relationship with someone else).

What is your reaction to reading this list? Do you think that none of these are possible for you? Does even the idea of any of these things cause you to feel upset, anxious, angry, depressed or even outraged?

Do you scoff at these alternatives and say to yourself:

"I couldn't possibly have <u>that</u>."

And does your mind come up with reasons why none of these are an option for you, such as:

- *"I love my spouse - I don't want anyone else."*

- *"I couldn't find anyone else better than my spouse."*

- *"I'm too old."*

- *"I'm too young."*

- *"There's no-one out there who could understand me like my spouse does."*

- *"Starting again in the dating game would be too difficult and stressful."*

- *"Starting again in my life would be too difficult and stressful."*

- *"I could never be happy if this marriage doesn't work."*

- *"I would struggle financially if our marriage ended."*

But are you 100% sure that all of these objections to alternatives to healing your marriage **are** true?

Or are they just things that you *think* **could** be true?

All of these objections really are nothing more than ideas in your head, aren't they?

For instance, you **could** meet someone tomorrow, unexpectedly, who turns out to be your new soulmate, who you love even more than your spouse.

It *is* theoretically possible, isn't it?

Instead of being fixated on the specific outcome of healing your marriage - instead of telling yourself that it is the only result that you will accept - tell yourself that, whatever happens in your life and your marriage, it is meant to be, and that things will turn out for the best.

What Happens When You Let Go

Once you trust that the best outcome for you will show up for you if you allow it to - and that it might be something that you can't currently see - you will find that good and unexpected things start happening in your life.

The first thing that happens is that you immediately begin to feel better. You release the pressure you have been putting on yourself.

By feeling better, you're more capable of handling any situation you're confronted with. And you're also more attractive to your spouse.

The next thing that happens is that you begin to become aware that the 'unseen power' I mentioned earlier really does exist.

You cease to feel so alone and powerless. You sense that this 'invisible power' wants the best for you and is guiding you towards it.

You may feel this power as a 'wise knowing' or an 'inner voice'. But whatever it is, you find yourself opening up to new ideas, opportunities and possibilities that are positive for your life.

This inner guiding power gives you intuitive ('gut') feelings about what you should and shouldn't do. As you begin to act on these feelings, you notice yourself getting better results and in an easier, happier way.

A third result of letting go is that most of the problems that you think you have, lessen or even disappear completely, as if by magic.

You may find yourself confronted by a 'crisis' or drama and the next day it has been resolved, perhaps by another person or events.

When you no longer push, struggle, and react to 'problems' - when you simply wait, confident and trusting, and only take action if and when it feels right (listening to your 'inner voice') - your spouse and other people react to you differently.

They treat you with more respect as they realize they you can't be manipulated or drawn into conflicts. The confidence and calm you project makes you someone they want to be with - and co-operate with - rather than a person they want to push against.

They become more reasonable to deal with. And they also take more responsibly for their own life, rather than trying to affect yours or blaming you for their circumstances.

You find yourself making better decisions. You do things more efficiently, with a lot less effort. You naturally do more of the right things and fewer of the wrong things.

Which of these would be more effective in helping to heal your marriage: saying the wrong thing twenty times, or saying the right thing three times?

Would you get a better result by complaining and criticizing twenty times or by saying something loving and positive three times?

When you let go, you'll find yourself doing three of the right things instead of twenty of the wrong things.

Your life will get a lot better, easier and more fulfilling when you let go of trying to force things to happen.

But as it says in the film The Matrix:

"I can only show you the door. You're the one who has to walk through it."

So, although you may accept what I have said about letting go, there may still be a part of you that is holding you back from actually doing it.

What is stopping you? Let's look at what it is......

What Stops You From Letting Go

Despite accepting on a theoretical level that letting go would give you better results, if you are like most people, you are probably struggling to 'take the leap of faith' and put it into practice in your own life.

Truly letting go is difficult, at least to begin with. And there is only one reason why (and you may have guessed this already). That reason is:

Fear.

Fear is what stops you from allowing the right things to come into your life. It stops you from trusting and letting go completely.

And fear is the underlying cause of not only all *your* problems and lack of happiness, but virtually all of the world's problems as well.

You love your wife or husband. You want your marriage to heal and return to the loving, joyful place it once was. You want it to be better than it has ever been.

But you are afraid that if you 'let go' of your marriage that you won't achieve that outcome. And that if you 'fail', 'bad things' will happen to you and your family.

You may be worried about what other people may think of you. You may be concerned about what you might think of yourself: that you didn't do everything that you could have to solve the problems and create a happy marriage. You may think that the rest of your life will be filled with unhappiness and regret.

All because you 'gave up' when just one more idea, technique or strategy could have turned everything around. You failed, when you were so close to success.....

These are just some of the thoughts that you have when you are afraid to let go and allow.

You will recall from earlier in this book that one of the most important things you need to heal your marriage is make the commitment to do "whatever it takes". As long as you continue to feel that your marriage is right for you, you must keep trying.

But are you truly prepared to do **whatever** it takes? Are you willing to do **anything** to achieve it?

Think carefully before you answer this. Because if your answer is 'Yes' then do this:

Stop trying to force your marriage to heal. Stop insisting that healing your marriage is the only thing you will accept.

Let go and allow whatever is best to happen.

Letting go of something to get it seems counterintuitive. And it is. Which is why so few people do it.

And it is the real reason why so few people succeed in getting what they want and are truly happy.

But it is the only thing that works, because letting go of your fears and trusting moves you from a negative energy state to a positive energy state. And from there you create positive results rather than negative ones.

Now that you know that letting go is the only way for the right things to happen in your life - and that the only thing stopping you from letting go is fear - the big question becomes:

"How do I stop being afraid?"

This is where the 'rubber hits the road' and it's what we'll look at next.

How to Eliminate Your Fears

Our deepest fears are like dragons guarding our deepest treasure.

- Rainer Maria Rilke

Most people have all sorts of underlying fears in their life, most of which they're not aware of. These fears hold them back, not only in their marriage, but in every other aspect of their life as well - their career or business, their health, their lifestyle, and their relationships with others.

And it is these fears which keep them stuck living a life way below their potential and being far less happy than they could (and should) be.

Of course, I am not talking about **all** fears here. Some fears are healthy, and in fact necessary for survival.

You **should** be afraid if someone is about to hit you, if you hear an explosion nearby, or if a fast-moving car is headed straight in your direction! These are real dangers.

But most of the things that cause you to feel fear are not real.

You are afraid of things that are imaginary - things that haven't happened and are probably unlikely to happen.

Because these fears are imaginary, they are irrational and unhelpful. And they need to be eliminated.

Removing fears is something that takes time and effort. You're not going to get rid of them straight away. After all, it has taken you a lifetime to accumulate those fears.

However, removing them can (and must) be done. Your happiness depends on it.

Here is a powerful four-step process that will help you to get rid of your imaginary and unhelpful fears - so that you can finally let go and experience the great life - and great marriage - you are designed to have.

Fear Elimination Process

Step #1: Identify your fears

Answer this question:

What are you afraid might happen - or not happen - if you don't heal your marriage?

Please spend some time on this. This is one of the most important questions for you to answer in this entire book.

Most of the time you are not aware of the fears that you hold within you. But even just 'bringing them to the surface of your mind' will dissipate a lot of their power.

Keep asking yourself this question and write down your answers. As you do so, more and more of your fears will be revealed to you.

Some of the most common fears that people have when answering this question include:

- Fear of being alone
- Fear of never find someone they could love as much
- Fear of feeling a failure
- Fear of regret
- Fear of financial hardship
- Fear of harming the children
- Fear of judgement and criticism by others
- Fear of not experiencing true love and intimacy
- Fear of living in a 'bad' marriage

If you have anything less than a perfect marriage, you will have some (or even all) of these fears.

Do your best to uncover as many of your fears as you can by continuing to ask yourself:

"What am I afraid might happen - or not happen - if I <u>don't</u> heal my marriage?"

Step #2: Play the Best Friend Game

For each of the fears that you have uncovered in Step #1 above, there is something very important to realize.

What you are afraid might happen isn't *guaranteed* (or even *likely*) to happen - your mind just *thinks* that it is.

In other words, it *looks like it will happen* - from your current perspective. But what *could* happen is only an **idea** held in your imagination. It's possible it could happen in the future, but it's not **actually** happening right now.

In other words, you are afraid of something that is not real.

The only reason why you feel afraid of it is because you see it as happening in your mind right now. But it is only 'happening' in your mind. Your mind makes it appear real.

To help you understand this more clearly, imagine you have a friend or family member who is struggling with their marriage, and who has come to you for support and advice.

A conversation with them might go something like this:

Friend: *"My spouse and I aren't getting along. They treat me badly; we haven't had sex for months and I'm totally miserable. I don't know what to do."*

You: *"It's obvious to me what you should do - don't put up with it. Move on. Leave. You and your spouse aren't really suited to each other anyway. Find someone else who is better."*

Friend: *"No I can't do that. Things used to be good in our marriage. I know we can work out our problems."*

You: *"But you have been complaining about your marriage for years. You both are on different planets! When are you going to realize it's never going to work out?"*

Friend: *"I just need to try a bit harder. I'm sure there is a way to solve our problems. I don't want to give up. I love them. I'll never find someone as good as them. Starting all over would be so difficult. I'm too old. There are a lot of strange people out there; all of the good ones are taken. I really don't have the time or energy to start looking for someone else. Besides, the children will be badly affected. They would be emotionally scarred, and the future would be very hard for them."*

In this scenario, **you** can clearly see what your friend should do.

You have a clear perspective on the truth about them and their situation.

But your friend has a different perspective. They can't see the truth: that they would be better off leaving and moving on to create a new life because their marriage is simply not right for them.

Your friend can't see what you see. And that is because of their fears. Their fears are literally blinding them to the truth.

This actually happens on a biological level. When you feel fear, your brain literally blocks your awareness of the right things to see and do in your life.

(If you would like to understand more about how your brain works to do this, check out my free podcast series, 'Using Your Brain for Success' which you will find on my website: www.liamnaden.com.)

But how would you continue this conversation with your friend? In all likelihood, you would try to convince them that what they are saying and thinking is simply **not true**.

You would use logic and reason, emotion, and even evidence - anything you could think of or find - to get them to see 'reality.' You might say something like:

"Why are you so afraid? You're a great person! Of course you would find someone as good! There are plenty of great single people out there, all looking for a great person such as you. You might meet a few "interesting" people along the way, but so what? If that happens, you just say "goodbye" and move on. It's all part of the adventure. And what do you mean you're too old? There are lots of great single people your age.

And your children will be perfectly fine - after all, they'd much rather see the two of you being happy rather than at each other's throats. There's lots of evidence out there to show that children brought up by loving (yet separated) parents turn out perfectly well. Stop being so afraid of the future. Everything will turn out great!"

If your friend still had objections, and if you really cared about them, you would probably want to continue the discussion until you convinced them that what you were saying was true. You wouldn't give up until they agreed with you.

And why wouldn't you give up until you succeeded? Because you care about them and are frustrated that they are blocking their own happiness with their false beliefs.

You know the truth about them and their marriage situation. You **know** how much happier they would be if they moved on from their marriage.

You can be masterful at helping others who you care about to overcome their irrational thoughts and fears.

But you need to apply the same strategy to help the person you care about the most. Your greatest friend of all:

Yourself.

So have the same conversation with **yourself** as you would with your closest friend!

For each of your fears that you identified, pretend that you are two people:

You are **Yourself**, with all of your fears and justifications.

And you are your **Best Friend**, someone who is determined to show you that whatever it is that you are afraid of is **not** true.

Have an imaginary conversation, with you playing the role of both of these people.

Play both sides of the argument, for and against each fear. Keep the conversation going until your Best Friend convinces Yourself that this fear is simply not true - that there is no way that it could be true. That it is nonsense! Impossible! Complete rubbish!

Like all games, the Best Friend Game can be fun. You can play the game as a verbal (or mental) conversation, or you could write the conversation down.

But also take this game seriously - because it is an extremely powerful way of getting rid of your fears. You'll realize that everything you were afraid of was nothing more than the result of wrong ideas that you had been putting in your head.

Step #3: Play the '*Then* What?' Game

If you enjoyed the game in Step #2, you're going to love the game in Step #3!

For each of the fears you identified in Step #1 - and which you now know are not only false but nonsensical (from Step #2) - ask yourself:

"If this happened, then what?"

Imagine yourself in a situation where the thing you are afraid **might** happen actually **did** happen.

Then what? What would happen next?

Come up with the very **next** thing you think would happen, and ask of that:

"Then what?"

Repeat for the next thing that you think would happen. Ask:

"Then what?"

Continue with this process. For every answer that comes to your mind, ask yourself:

"Then what?"

When you start this conversation, most of the answers you get will probably be negative - things that you don't want to happen.

But keep going and what you will find is that you eventually come up with positive things. It is then that you will see that even if what you are afraid of **did** actually happen, eventually it would result in a positive outcome for you.

In other words, even if the thing that you are afraid of happened, it would still be of benefit to you. It would simply be a step along the road towards a much happier life.

Here's an example, again using the fear that you will 'never find anyone else as good as your spouse for a relationship'.

The conversation with yourself could go something like this:

"I will never find another person I could love as much as my spouse."

"Then what?"

"I would be on my own, feeling lonely, really missing my spouse and regretting the end of our marriage."

"Then what?"

"I'd be sad, not having anyone to share my life or be intimate with."

"Then what?"

"I'd spend my time talking to myself and trying to make the best of things on my own."

"Then what?"

"I'd get tired of being on my own eventually and I would spend a bit more time with friends."

"Then what?"

"They would encourage me to meet new people and to find a new romantic relationship."

"Then what?"

"I'd start looking for a new romance. I'd be open to meeting new people. I'd probably sign up for a couple of social and dating websites."

"Then what?"

"I'd put up a profile online of what I was looking for. And I'd go on a few dates and/or go to some social events."

"Then what?"

"I'd meet some interesting new people and expand my social circle."

"Then what?"

"I'd meet someone who I really connected with and form a great new relationship with them."

"Then what?"

"I'd be enjoying life more than I ever had before!"

Can you see what is happening here? You're coming to see the truth - that what you are afraid of is in fact a step towards a truly happy and great life!

And while things might be a bit rocky for a while, eventually everything will turn out much better for you.

Step #4: Switch to Power Thinking

If you have put some effort into these steps, by now your fears should be losing much of their power. But you probably won't get rid of them completely overnight. After all, they took a long time to get into your head in the first place!

There may be times when these fears come back and feel like they are overpowering you. You may become anxious, worried and even panicky.

But even if these fears do 'get to you' from time to time, know that they **are** losing their power over you.

However, there is another thing that you can do during these times of doubt and anxiety. It's one of the most powerful things of all.

It's what I call **Power Thinking**.

And it comes from asking yourself one of the best questions you could ever ask yourself:

"What could I be grateful for about my life right now?"

Most people become so caught up in their fears and problems that they completely lose the perspective on who they really are and how their life really is.

But gratitude acts like a switch in your mind. It switches you from negative to positive energy. From illusion to truth.

When you are grateful for your life as it is, you not only feel better, but you open your mind to see the truth of who you really are.

You have so much to be grateful for! You are an amazing person! You are experiencing an amazing life!

Your life is better than that of most people on this planet - and better than that of nearly every person who has **ever** lived.

You have your family, people who love you. You have your health. You have life comforts that you enjoy which only a few years ago weren't available to anyone on earth (and still aren't available to many).

You have the gift of life itself.

And through being here right now - reading this book - you are learning things about how to improve your life that few people ever learn.

In fact, I know that if you have picked up this book and put in the effort to have read this far that you are a very special person.

You are indeed an incredible individual - and so lucky to be here! So ask yourself:

"What could I be grateful for about my life right now?"

And whatever answers you get, focus on those things for a few seconds or minutes. You don't need to write them down. Just reflect mentally on the blessings you have in your life as it is right now.

Switch your thinking from fear to gratitude and you will step into a power you didn't know you had. And your life will change massively for the better.

* * *

These four steps will help you see the truth about who you are, what your life is really like and what you need to do to solve your problems and create the life and loving relationship that you love and deserve.

And you will finally feel the joy and relief that comes from getting rid of the only thing which has been holding you back and stopping you from having a great life all this time: your fears.

The Magic of Letting Go

I said earlier that when you let go, things start to happen in your life as if by magic. And there really is a magic attached to it.

Things will begin to happen for you that will be both unexpected and great!

New and better people will show up in your life. Problems will go away or resolve themselves.

You will make better decisions. You will take better actions. New ideas will come to you. New information that can help you will come your way.

And you'll realize the truth that life really is meant to be a wonderful adventure, not a perpetual struggle.

And whether you heal your marriage or go on to your next adventure in a different direction, you'll end up in the best place for you.

You will become the happiest and best version of yourself that you can be.

And that is the real reason why you are here.

Final Thoughts

A loving relationship with another person is one of the most special and unique things a human can experience.

Yet it is one of the great tragedies in the world today that so few people ever get to know the true depth of love in their marriage that they are capable of.

This is because that what we have been taught about relationships - and how to create and nurture them - is mostly wrong.

We have been led to believe that marriage is difficult and needs to be 'worked on'. That problems are inevitable. That we should be happy with what we have because 'no marriage is perfect'.

In completing this book, you now know that none of these things are true.

Instead, you understand that all you need for a great marriage is to become the person who is worthy of it.

In other words, you need to focus on developing *you*.

The more you do this, the more you bring out the true goodness and beauty that is the essence of who you really are.

And the more you will see that reflected in your outside world, including in your marriage.

You are a wonderful and perfect person! And when you know that is true, you will have a wonderful and perfect marriage.

My wish for you is that you get what you deserve - the very best!

Liam Naden

Key Concepts

The 6 Foundations of Uncounseling

1. Understanding who you really are
2. Knowing what you really want
3. Understanding your spouse
4. Being attractive
5. Being an effective communicator
6. Being fearless

The 6 Natural Principles of Marriage

1. Whatever you focus on you get more of.
2. You can't fix your marriage; you can only fix yourself.
3. The relationship that you have with your spouse is a reflection of the relationship that you have with yourself.
4. You - and you alone - are responsible for how you feel and for every result you get in your life.
5. Nothing means anything other than the meaning you choose to give it.
6. True power comes not from trying to force a specific result, but from allowing the right result to appear.

Definitions

- **Perfect Marriage**: A marriage in which your emotional needs are met.
- **Mistake**: A Learning Experience that improves the quality of your life.
- **Effective Communication**: Not the result of what you say but the result of what the other person understands.

The Marriage Success Mindset

1. *"I am going to heal our marriage. It feels right. I love my spouse and I'll do whatever it takes for us to do this."*
2. *"I am a great person, worthy of love and of having a happy and fulfilling life."*
3. *"I create my own happiness."*
4. *"I am not dependent on my marriage for me to be happy."*
5. *"I am attractive, physically, mentally, emotionally and sexually. I work on becoming more attractive every day."*
6. *"I focus on the positive aspects of our marriage."*
7. *"Our marriage can and will get better."*

The 4 Keys to Marriage Success

1. Stay positive
2. Love your spouse unconditionally
3. Focus on your own self worth
4. Keep your goal in mind

The Marriage Uncounseling Action Checklist

Yourself:

- Work on yourself - not on your spouse or your marriage
- Put yourself first - not last
- Take responsibility for your marriage situation - don't blame anyone or anything else
- Eliminate your fears - don't allow your fears to control you

Your Focus:

- On what you want - not what you don't want
- On the good in your relationship - not the problems
- On the good in your life - not the problems
- On the good in everything that happens and has happened - not the bad
- On the present and the future - not the past

Your Actions:

- Praise - don't criticize
- Agree - don't disagree
- Be attractive - not unattractive
- Laugh - don't cry
- Smile - don't frown
- Be optimistic - not pessimistic
- Be patient - not impatient
- Allow - don't force
- Trust - don't be afraid

Free Bonuses

With this book you have everything you need to create a very special marriage for you and your spouse, no matter how things are at the moment.

However, sometimes you may find yourself getting stuck or wanting things to happen more quickly.

That's why I have included some free additional resources for you. Each of these will give you an extra edge in creating the ideal marriage you really want and deserve to have.

And by the way, all of these bonuses are exclusive to this book. I don't offer them anywhere else.

Free Bonus #1: The Five Ultimate Love Letters Collection

These unique letters contain words and ideas I have used with my private coaching clients and they have proven to be very effective.

Choose the letter that is most appropriate for your situation and send it to your spouse by email or text - or be really romantic and write it inside a card and give it to them with or without a gift.

Be sure to change the text of the letter so that it is personal to you.

Love Letter #1: 'Attraction Activator'

If you do everything suggested in chapter 5 you will certainly see a big improvement in the attraction in your marriage.

But if you really want to turbocharge things, you can use this special 'Attraction Activator' Letter.

Don't worry - there's nothing shocking or raunchy in this letter. But it does contain some ideas that will get your spouse's juices flowing again....

Love Letter #2: 'True Forgiveness'

Your spouse may feel deeply hurt by what has happened in your marriage and find it very difficult to forgive.

In this letter, you can show them a new way to look at forgiveness and to feel safe to let go of their hurt and pain.

This is a very loving letter....and it will touch your spouse in a profound way.

Love Letter #3: 'Open Communication'

Sometimes, no matter what you do, you still feel that communication could be better in your relationship. It can seem like there is still a 'wall' between you.

This letter will help you to break down that wall. It will help open up your spouse's willingness to connect with you on a deeper and more meaningful level.

Love Letter #4: 'Love and Appreciation'

It is often difficult to express love and appreciation for your spouse in a way that will touch them deeply. This is especially true when your marriage is encountering difficulties.

Use this letter to show your spouse just how much they mean to you. It will remind them of just how special your marriage is.

Love Letter #5: 'Change Your Mind'

If all seems lost in your marriage, if your spouse simply refuses to co-operate with you, if they want to leave or even if they have already left - this is a very powerful letter that can help them to change their mind.

This letter is no substitute for doing the work I've presented you with in this book. But use it if all else fails. The words in this letter may just save your marriage.

Free Bonus #2: Book Summary

This summary will give you a quick overview of the most important points in this book. It will help you get clear on the best ways to use the information for your specific marriage situation.

Free Bonus #3: Inner Circle Membership

From time to time I produce additional material to help you dive deeper into your marriage. When you claim the above free bonuses you will automatically become part of an exclusive group where I share this information first.

You'll get first access to online events and unique content. I will also be sending you even more free resources from time to time. I look forward to staying in touch.

Get all of these free bonuses right now at:

www.marriageuncounselingbonuses.com

About the Author

Liam Naden has been helping couples and individuals save and heal their marriage for more than a decade.

He is the host of the podcast: 'Growing in Love for Life: Save and Strengthen Your Marriage' and author of several books.

Liam is also the creator of several highly acclaimed and effective coaching programs.

He spends his time speaking, teaching, writing and researching on how to improve any marriage or relationship, no matter what the current circumstances.

More Help

If you would like more help to succeed in your marriage and your life check out my coaching programs below.

They are available at www.liamnaden.com

The 9 Habits for an Unshakeable Marriage

All great marriages share in common 9 simple habits. Learn what they are and how you too can use them to make your marriage last.

Stop Your Divorce - Even if Your Spouse Doesn't Want To (7 day program)

A program specifically designed for individuals and couples who are facing divorce. You will learn a quick and powerful method to get your spouse interested in you and your marriage again.

Save Your Marriage: 30 Days to Relationship Transformation

This is a revolutionary system specifically designed for those who are facing the agony of their marriage ending. You will learn how to overcome past hurts, rekindle your love and build a healthy, strong marriage for the future.

- Includes advanced methods for deep attraction, communication and forgiveness.
- Also suitable for couples wanting to heal their marriage and create ever-deeper intimacy and love.
- An ideal complement to the Stop Your Divorce - Even if Your Spouse Doesn't Want To program.

Happy Blended Families (for stepparents and children)

This program will help you create a truly harmonious and loving blended family so that you *all* move forward and create a wonderful life together.

Stop all the conflict and drama in your blended family (stepfamily) - quickly, easily and for good!

Get Past Your Breakup (7 day program)

This program will enable you get over the pain and heartache of the end of your marriage or relationship and move forward in your life as the best version of *you*.

Re-Balance Your Brain for Success (with Neuro-State Rebalancing) - a life success program

Understand how your brain works and how to use it to bring you everything you really want. You will learn to 'reset' your brain for success using a method called Neuro-State Rebalancing (NSR).

All available at www.liamnaden.com

Made in United States
Orlando, FL
08 January 2023

28403846R00098